A Visitor's Guide to
Jonathan Dickinson
State Park

By James D. Snyder

Sponsored by Friends of Jonathan Dickinson State Park

WELCOME TO

JONATHAN DICKINSON STATE PARK

Pharos
Books
Jupiter, Florida

TABLE OF CONTENTS

A Visitor's Guide to Jonathan Dickinson State Park,
including 12 maps and 173 photographs. Written by James D. Snyder.

Copyright 2009 © Friends of Jonathan Dickinson State Park, Inc.

Published by **Pharos Books** on behalf of :
the **Friends of Jonathan Dickinson State Park, Inc.,**
a non-profit community service organization at:

16450 S. E. Federal Highway,
Hobe Sound, FL 33455.
Phone: 561-744-9814.
friendsofjdsp.org

Graphic Design by Rebecca Barbier, Englewood, Florida.
beckoecko@aol.com

First printing, first edition. Printed in South Korea.

ISBN 978-0-9675200-8-7

Front cover photography by Judy Norton, from a collection of photos taken as a volunteer in the park for
over ten years. Her glimpses of "the magical and primordial" scenes along the river's edge have been exhibited
in the museums of the Loxahatchee River Historical Society, the MacArthur Beach (FL) State Park and the
A.E. Bean Backus Museum and Gallery in Fort Pierce, FL. For information about individual photos in the
collection, contact Judy Norton at mindshower@bellsouth.net.

Inside cover photo (and photo below) by Cecelia Trevejo Shutan, a Los Angeles, CA portrait photographer.
She encountered this couple canoeing on Kitching Creek during her first visit to the park in January 2009.

This booklet was written with the sponsorship and help of the Friends of Jonathan Dickinson State Park. One of the reasons the members of this non-profit organization love our park is that it is an oasis of calm sandwiched between rapidly growing towns: Jupiter-Tequesta to the South and Stuart and Hobe Sound to the North. Within these 11,500 acres are a wild and scenic river and the same wildlife that were seen by generations of Native Americans, pioneer growers and railroad builders. And for many, the park is a poignant part of our own family histories. We come here to enjoy, to reflect and to remember.

We hope you will, too. We want to be sure you're aware of all the activities available. And we think you'll enjoy them even more if you know something about the park's history, its ecology and some of the issues that park managers face in trying to preserve its wild and scenic nature.

James D. Snyder
Pharos Books
Jupiter, FL

A View That Spans Centuries

Most folks think of South Florida as too "new" to have much history. After all, its oldest building (Jupiter Inlet Lighthouse) is only approaching 150 years. As recently as a century ago, the entire 250-mile coastal strip from Titusville to Key Biscayne contained barely a thousand people.

But now take another look! Start your visit to Jonathan Dickinson State Park by climbing the tower atop Hobe Mountain and you'll see why.

Look west and you'll gaze on much the same undisturbed landscape that ancient Indians did at least 5,000 years ago.

Look east to the ocean and see where Spanish galleons glided on the Gulf Stream on their way to Spain with gold and silver from South America.

Southeast, just beyond your gaze, is Jupiter Inlet, which was entered by Ponce de León in 1513.

Looking south, many of the east-west highways cover the original trails used by Seminole Indians and their U. S. Army pursuers in the mid-nineteenth century.

Look down right below you and imagine an army base with 7,000 men and 400 structures springing up almost overnight in 1942. Then imagine the whole complex just a few years later: a ghost camp of concrete slabs.

The Native American centuries

Several centuries before the Spanish explorer Ponce de León arrived at Jupiter Inlet, Indians were using the trails and river in today's state park. Because these early Indians (not to be confused with the later Seminoles) left no sign of a written language, it's difficult to pinpoint how long they lived in any one area or who ruled what domain. A rough sketch would show the large Calusa kingdom based around Estero Bay (near Fort Myers). A second was the Miaymi, who lived around the rim of Lake Okeechobee. Smaller groups – perhaps sub-clans or vassals of the first two – included the Aiys around Indian River Inlet, the Jeaga at Jupiter Inlet and the Tequesta where Miami is today.

The Jeaga of Jupiter Inlet were blessed with an abundance of food, so that the planting of crops was rare. Great schools of fish swam along the beach. Giant loggerhead turtles crawled ashore in summertime and laid delicious eggs. Pools by the inlets teemed with snook and the river exploded with swarms of mullet. Estuaries were full of clams and the mangrove roots held an endless supply of oysters. It was also easy to dig out and dam up fish ponds so as to keep live fish and turtles.

On land, deer abounded and bear were common. Wild fruits such as pond apple and berries such as the saw palmetto added zest to the subtle change of seasons. In the rivers upstream were manatee, alligators and otters.

Regardless of their political structure, the Indian tribes of South Florida shared common traits. These hunter-gatherers made fire and cooked with pottery vessels. And like the Midwestern Indians known as "mound builders," they erected sand and earth mounds for their temples and graves.

However, their civilization was unique because their implements were largely limited to those they found in South Florida. Lacking flints for arrow heads, they made deadly arrows of hard reeds and sharpened them in fire. The soft Florida limestone was useless for hammers and axes, but the Indians found dozens of ways to use the wealth of shells they found on beaches. Most valuable was the giant conch, which they drilled with holes and lashed with deer gut to make strong wooden handles for picks and shovels. Smaller conch shells were used as jewelry or weights for fishing nets.

At home, it was the job of women to cook and make pottery. Unlike many early peoples, a typical piece of pottery was decorated only with simple lines or checks — perhaps merely as a way to identify its owner. But the men, apparently with more time on their hands, made intricate shell and wood carvings. Using shark teeth, set in wood handles, they carved the outer conch shells with wavy lines as jewelry to hang on long strands from their belts. Their finest carving was done in the wood of pond apple or mangrove tree. They might make images of gods for dancers to wear on masks in their religious processions. Or they might produce wooden plaques with animal heads identifying their clan. These would be set on long poles around houses or high on a palmetto-thatched temple.

One reason it's hard to pin down the domain of a given tribe is that it moved around depending on the season or hunting conditions. For example, in the summer when insects could become thick inland, whole villages would travel to the beach to feel the cool breeze, feast on oysters or go hunting in the ocean for game fish.

In the 16th century, when gold-laden Spanish fleets began to ride the Gulf Stream towards home in late summer and early fall, Indians had another reason to come to the beach. Sometimes it was to trade when the passers-by sent launches in for water and sometimes to plunder a wrecked ship. Although the Indians had no practical use for gold (except to admire how it glittered in the sun) they soon realized it could be traded for items they truly valued – kettles, knives, hatchets and other "modern" conveniences of the day.

It was in this context that Jonathan Dickinson State Park got its name. In 1696 England was beginning to challenge Spain's domination of South Florida when the schooner *Reformation*, owned by a leading Philadelphia family, ran aground on Jupiter Island about five miles north of today's inlet. The Jeaga Indians who lived along the inlet were loyal to the Spanish and proceeded to make life miserable for Jonathan Dickinson and the 26 English colonists who survived the wreck. It was only through their wits — and devout prayer, as the Quaker Dickinson described it — that the party was spared and sent on a harrowing march up the shoreline that ended weeks later in the hands of the more tolerant Spanish at St. Augustine. Out of this grueling experience came

GODS

PROTECTING   PROVIDENCE
MAN'S
SUREST HELP AND DEFENCE
In the times
Of the greatest difficulty and most Imminent danger;
Evidenced in the

Remarkable Deliverance

Of divers Persons,
From the devouring Waves of the Sea, amongst which
they Suffered Shipwrack.
And also
From the more cruelly devouring jawes of the inhumane
CANIBALS of FLORIDA.
Faithfully related by one of the persons concerned therein;
JONATHAN DICKENSON.

Psal. 93 : 4. *The Lord on high is mightier than the noise of many Waters,
yea than the mighty Waves of the Sea.*
Psal. 74 : 20. *The dark places of the Earth are full of the habitations
of Cruelty.*

Printed in *Philadelphia* by *Reinier Jansen.* 1699.

The cover of Jonathan Dickinson's best selling book about his ordeal.

a book by Dickinson that became a best seller for years in America and Europe.

In 1950, when officials in Tallahassee asked the leaders of tiny Hobe Sound what they should name their new state park, they came up with a name associated with the most memorable local event they could recall. And that's how Jonathan Dickinson State Park wound up with a name that had nothing to do with anything within its boundaries!

Well, almost. Many early Spanish charts contain a marker for ships passing Hobe Sound. They cited Hobe Mountain in the park as the "Bleach Yard." Translation: before the old dune grew vegetation, its glistening white sugar sands reminded sailors of billowing sails left out to dry. And so it became a landmark for navigators.

The Seminole era

In 1783, as part of the treaty that ended the Revolutionary War, England took possession of Florida. By that time, there weren't enough left of the once flourishing Calusa, Miaymi, Aiys or Jeaga to care much what white people did in South Florida. European diseases and/or slavers had all but wiped out an Indian population that may have reached 20,000 in its prime. When the Spanish prepared to abandon their capital of St. Augustine, they rounded up all the indigenous Indians they could find so as to ship them off to Cuba to work in the sugar fields. They could locate no more than a hundred souls.

During the next thirty or so years, South Florida nearly reverted to a primitive, pristine wilderness. There were no roads and no port for ships to enter. The waterways again became the province of mosquitoes, mangroves and manatee. Bears, panthers and alligators ruled the land. They were joined by two accidents of history. The Spanish had lacked enough ships on their exodus to Cuba and had to leave behind many cattle, hogs and horses. These castoffs soon began to multiply in the plains and pine woods of South Florida.

The stage was now set for another human incursion. The young, swaggering United States was becoming The Promised Land for eager European immigrants, all expecting cheap homesteads in a land of unlimited opportunity. In border states like Alabama, Georgia and South Carolina, Cherokees and other native tribes found themselves chased away from their ancestral lands by people who waved pieces of paper in their faces claiming themselves as the owners. Indians (who believed that the land belonged to everyone) found themselves heading south into the territory of Florida. Sometimes they were joined by African slaves who had escaped from southern plantations.

The two peoples had something to offer one another. The Indians generally knew how to manage animals, and

SEMINOLE INDIANS   FLORIDA

Scene of the Battle of the Loxahatchee, just off Indiantown Road

they were soon becoming America's first cowboys as they began to herd the wild Spanish cattle. The escaped slaves often had farming skills, which the Indians hadn't bothered much about. Before long the two had reached a workable modus vivendi: the Indians "officially" would be owners of the escaped slaves, but the latter would live in their own agricultural villages, almost unrestricted except for the obligation to pay their Indian protectors part of their harvest.

This arrangement was working pretty well during the 1820s when Anglo-European farmers began pressing into Florida as well. Again, the white farmers saw the Indians and Africans as a faceless amalgam of dark skinned peoples and began calling them "Seminoles," Spanish slang for "runaways" or "fugitives."

During this time, a few white settlers grew sugar and citrus along the Indian River north of Jupiter Inlet. Like other Florida farmers, they often clashed with the Seminoles.

The more that leaders in Washington heard about conflict in Florida, the more agitated they became. The U.S. had forgiven Spain $5 million in debts in exchange for the territory, and Congress expected a return on its "investment" from farming and commerce. Before long Washington was aflame with debate on how to contain the "Seminole threat" and an army of 4,000 was raised to march into South Florida, round up the offending Indians (who numbered no more than 4,000 counting women and children) and send them out west to reservations.

In January 1838, where Indiantown Road crosses the river in Riverbend Park, the Battle of the Loxahatchee was fought, effectively ending the Second Seminole Indian War. Although some 300 Seminoles actually ambushed a U.S. army force during a march down the well-worn military trail towards Jupiter Inlet, the half-starved Indians were beaten back by overwhelming numbers and eventually forced to surrender. Some of the archeological sites in Riverbend and Jonathan Dickinson parks relate to that bloody and decisive battle.

How a railroad changed the region

In the years afterward, vegetation reclaimed the old military trails, the wooden stockade forts collapsed and the area around the Loxahatchee remained almost unsettled. Even when a lighthouse was built at Jupiter Inlet in 1860, the lack of roads or railroads meant that tons of materials had to be off-loaded 35 miles north at Fort Pierce Inlet and hauled down the Indian River by barge.

A turn of the century paddlewheeler, perhaps "quarters" for a logging surveryor.

By 1890 steamboats were plying the Indian River from Titusville to Jupiter, and in that year entrepreneurs built a narrow-gauge, one-track rail line linking Jupiter and the tip of Lake Worth, seven miles to the south. Now farmers were beginning to rim the 22-mile lake and at its hub was a little town that would become Palm Beach. But farmers still faced a big handicap. They had to rely on steamboats and ox carts to bring their crops to the nearest rail line in Jacksonville, and often the produce arrived bruised or rotten. Henry Flagler, who had already amassed a $500 million fortune as John D. Rockefeller's right hand man at Standard Oil, vacationed in nearby St. Augustine one winter and quickly grasped an opportunity calling for the kind of investment that very few could afford. He determined to build a railroad down the east coast of Florida all the way to a southern terminus where his line could receive shiploads of cheap pineapples from Cuba and goods from South America.

In 1893, when Flagler's Florida East Coast Railway opened a station in Jupiter, it quickly put the little seven-mile Celestial Railway out of business. But for everyone else along the new tracks it was as if Henry Flagler had personally watered the economy with buckets of greenbacks. He invested in local businesses and gave to church building projects. People who had eked out hardscrabble farming now had access to markets as far up the coast as Boston. They raised ferns for floral arrangements and planted acres of tomatoes. In the scrubland ridges (including today's parkland bordering on U.S. Highway 1) they grew pineapples and hauled them by mule cart to the railway station in Jupiter. The poorest of farmers would go out in the pine woods, cut down trees and stack them beside the tracks. Train engineers would stop and load the bundles because they needed the wood to fuel their steam engines. They also needed lumber for the enormous 1,500-room Royal Poinciana Hotel that Flagler was building in Palm Beach.

As the 20th century approached, logging was becoming more mechanized within the lands that would one day become the state park. One of the loggers was a B. K. Hunt who built a home and two-stack sawmill on the Loxahatchee. Reports the late historian Bessie Dubois:

He went along the river and girdled the huge cypress trees a year before he began his operations. Then he went in with his oxen and some kind of pincers with which he pulled the trees down. They floated them on a catamaran down to the sawmill.

I know that the saw mill operated until about 1895. Mr. Hunt had a quarrel with a man named Bennefield, who owned the high property up on Kitching Creek. He got so angry with Mr. Hunt that he threatened either to kill him or burn his sawmill down. Shortly thereafter the saw mill did burn down and he (Bennefield) was the prime suspect. He received ten years in the penitentiary. The sawmill was gone and that ended the logging operation – for a while.

Fishing upriver, 1920s.

In the 1930s, when folks did most anything to survive the Depression, itinerant cypress cutters roamed the area. The loggers, in teams of 20, would literally wheel a steam engine — sometimes pulled by horses — out in the woods. Power from the steam boiler would run a large leather fan belt with a rotary saw blade at the other end. Once the crew had leveled everything saleable within a mile or so radius and stacked it into planks, the whole operation would move on to another strand of cypress or other hardwoods.

Sometimes when a worn-out steam engine was left behind, locals would find it in the woods and convert it to a moonshine still. Today there's the husk of an old Frick steam boiler rusting away near Kitching Creek.

It's also no coincidence that, except for the canopied stretch above Trapper Nelson's camp, the most accessible stand of bald cypress can be seen along the trail along Kitching Creek. Bessie Dubois and her family, who ran a fish camp and restaurant down by the Inlet, owned 37 acres along Kitching Creek that they used mostly for Sunday outings. Again, as Bessie told it:

Sizing up a cypress.

A glimpse of the toll taken by logging.

In 1941 the Loxahatchee was logged again. A man by the name of Arbuthnot was an unusual person because he was blind, having lost his sight in a sawmill accident. He did sawmilling from the back of the (Dubois) property and had a gas tramway. He cut down pine and cypress. We didn't want the cypress to be cut around our Kitching Creek property, so my husband marked the trees that should not be cut. He went up with a bucket of white paint and marked 27 trees around our camp and they were saved.

Trapper (in pith helmet) with a troupe of eager tourists.

Jupiter's own 'Tarzan'

Nearly ten miles upstream from Jupiter Inlet, amidst a magnificent stand of old trees, lived a "hermit" who would become known far beyond his remote riverside haunt. His name was Vincent Natulkiewicz and he was born in 1908 to recent Polish immigrants in Trenton, N.J. As a rambunctious teenager, already filling out a muscular physique on a six foot two inch frame, he began to ride the rails with his brother in what would be years of hoboing and trapping across the country.

In 1934 or thereabouts, Natulkiewicz came back to the one place where he had found more water, game, fish — and privacy — than anywhere else. By then he had changed his name to Vince Nelson. At dockside down at the Dubois fish camp, he bought a stout rowboat and filled it with tackle, ropes, traps and tools. He rowed the bulky boat upstream and didn't stop until he'd gone to where the current goes fast around a canopied bend. There he found the foundation of some long-abandoned cabin.

Every week or so he would row back down river for provisions. By then he was known simply as "Trapper Nelson," and folks would stop what they were doing when he strode down the Dubois dock wearing only shorts and hunting boots. Tarzan movies were all the rage at the local cinema and this fellow looked better than the one in Hollywood!

Folks also wondered what was going on up in that wilderness camp of his. Rumor had it that he tamed rattlesnakes, ate possum for dinner and wrestled alligators. Not having much else to do in a Depression-era town of a couple hundred, those who could afford gas for their motor boats would arrive at Trapper's camp unannounced with a picnic basket and something to assuage their host's famous appetite.

What the first arrivals found was an impressive cleared camp with a long dock, timbered cabin and large chickee hut. Above a shed was a crude, galvanized metal water tower connected to pipes that irrigated a large garden containing everything from pineapples to tomatoes. Hanging over the

river from a fat tree limb was a long rope that would swing you out into the deep, clear river. And you could gulp down cool, clean water as you swam back to shore.

Vince Nelson went trapping every morning. But so many picnickers were now showing up in the afternoons that it wasn't long before a large sign went up: *Trapper's Zoo and Jungle Garden.* Another hand-painted sign on a tree read: *Adults 50¢. Children 25¢.* What had been a self-sustaining farmette now sported hand-built cages containing alligators, rattlesnakes, wildcats, panthers and unusual specimens such as an albino raccoon. Along the dock, extended to 150 feet to accommodate tour boats,

were items for sale: air plants, animal skeletons, baby alligators, pineapples and bamboo fishing poles.

From then on Trapper Nelson was one-third trapper, one-third showman/yarn spinner, and one-third property acquirer. He watched keenly for county lists of landowners who were delinquent in paying taxes, and he scooped up parcels of 40 or so acres at a time for as low as $2 an acre. Over four decades he would amass more than 1,100 acres of prime riverfront property, and after his mysterious death in 1968, some 856 acres of it would be annexed to the park and play a pivotal role in preserving the upper Loxahatchee.

The rifle range at Camp Murphy. The sand hills beyond it are still full of spent shells.

Camp Murphy erupts in the sand and scrub

In 1942 everyone in and around what became today's state park was in for a rude interruption. After the Japanese invaded Pearl Harbor, people who had squatted on land west of U.S. 1 — the descendants of those early pineapple growers — were told by the federal government they must leave. Trapper Nelson soon found himself in an army boot camp, leaving behind a new bride who didn't last long at feeding rattlesnakes and alligators all by herself. On Kitching Creek, the Dubois family and other small landowners found their properties confiscated by the same government officials who tossed out the folks along Route 1.

What was going on? All locals knew was that something like 11,000 acres was needed for some kind of top-secret operation. If they'd gone down to Riviera Beach, snuck past the guards and peered inside some old boat warehouses, they would have seen a group of U.S. Army Signal Corps men hunched over what looked like amateur radios. Actually, they were putting the final touches on a revolutionary development called radar (for radio detecting and ranging). With it they could get a jump on locating bombing targets and incoming enemy aircraft. It could even be the key to winning the war.

What the Signal Corps needed now was a base on which to train thousands of radar operators — and quickly. Many of the squatters along U.S. 1 probably hadn't realized that most of the 11,000 or so acres were actually owned by the Hobe Sound Company, which was controlled by the Reed family of Jupiter Island. The Reeds sold 7,996 acres to the government and leased another 3,368 acres on condition that it would be properly restored after the war.

Armed with the mandate for all those acres, the cramped cadre in Riviera Beach busted out to the new campus in April 1942. Within something like 90 days Camp Col. William H. Murphy (named for the highest ranking Signal Corps officer to be killed in combat at the time) sprang to life and was officially christened on July 5. Spread mostly along the scrubland around U.S. 1 was a self-contained city of more than 400 structures, built to accommodate 854 officers and 5,742 enlisted men. The cost: $5.3 million.

Also known as the Southern Signal Corps School, it was the first training post built under a War Department plan calling for a "dispersed layout" or "theater of war." This meant that buildings were usually painted green and camouflaged by extensive replanting of bamboo, southern pine and other tropical vegetation. Little did passers-by on U.S. 1 know that the tightly-guarded base had its own railroad spur (for coal and freight), water/sewer system, power plant, bank, movie theater, church, mess hall and bowling alley. Today's Pine Grove Campground, in fact, is built right where the Camp Murphy hospital once stood.

And one thing more. Signal Corps soldiers didn't just sit in offices behind the line of fire. Often they advanced well ahead of the main body of troops so they could radio enemy positions to field commanders. If they were discovered they had to know how to defend themselves, and that meant learning how to handle rifles and machine guns at Camp Murphy. This also explains why such a large parcel was needed for training. When a raw recruit began spraying 50-caliber machine gun bullets in an arc, one needed plenty of empty land behind the firing range. It also explains why visitors still uncover shell casings around the old "Machine Gun Hill."

Once Camp Murphy's trainees settled in, they realized that a lot besides buildings had been camouflaged. Due to the stifling heat and lack of air conditioning, most radar classes began at 6 p.m. Snakes visited the barracks at night. Because Jupiter was usually deadsville for fun seekers on weekend passes, most stayed on base Saturday nights where they were joined by local girls for U.S.O. dances. The entire Dubois family worked at the camp in various positions and Bessie baked two dozen pies for the commissary almost every day.

Over at the camp infirmary, the biggest cause of patient visits in the first months of Camp Murphy wasn't stray bullets, but bites from snakes and black widow spiders. And this may help explain a strange coincidence. Joseph Reed, who had furnished the land for the camp, and who had managed to enlist as its "officer in charge of camp morale," had made many visits to Trapper Nelson's Zoo and Jungle Garden with his family and houseguests before the war. Now he learned that Trapper was sulking in his Mississippi boot camp while nursing an accidental wound in the thigh.

Within a few weeks, Private Vince Nelson was transferred to Camp Murphy

Map of Camp Murphy, 1942-44

and put in charge of "predator control." He would spend his hours chasing black widow spiders across the mess hall and plunking them in a box. Rattlers and other scary snakes would be grabbed and stuffed into a gunny sack. And off Trapper would go in his army Jeep to his riverfront hideaway, where his latest prizes would be added to his tourist menagerie. The Jeep proved also handy in ferrying soldiers out to his place on weekends for all-night poker games.

Just as Trapper was beginning to make big poker money and Bessie Dubois was wondering how she could keep baking so many pies, the curtain fell on Camp Murphy almost as fast as it had risen. The Signal Corps' other radar school was in Fort Monmouth, N.J. and in 1944, army brass suddenly decided that it could handle all training needs for the rest of the war. On November 30, the Hobe Sound base was officially decommissioned.

What would happen to the 400 buildings that popped up on the scrubland? The federal government got first choice and carted off tins of food, tools and similar supplies to other camps. The state of Florida was next in line, and took mostly fixtures from buildings. After a few

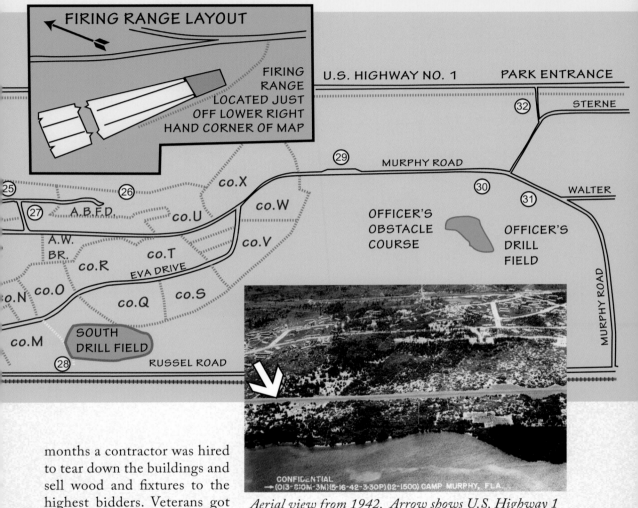

FIRING RANGE LAYOUT

FIRING RANGE LOCATED JUST OFF LOWER RIGHT HAND CORNER OF MAP

U.S. HIGHWAY NO. 1   PARK ENTRANCE

STERNE

MURPHY ROAD

WALTER

co.X
co.W
co.U
co.V
A.B.F.D.
A.W. BR.
co.T
co.R
EVA DRIVE
co.O
co.N
co.Q
co.S
co.M
SOUTH DRILL FIELD
RUSSEL ROAD

OFFICER'S OBSTACLE COURSE
OFFICER'S DRILL FIELD
MURPHY ROAD

Aerial view from 1942. Arrow shows U.S. Highway 1

months a contractor was hired to tear down the buildings and sell wood and fixtures to the highest bidders. Veterans got first choice, but not that many appeared with cash in hand. Before long termites, spores, and other subtropical gremlins began to eat away at the wood faster than the contractor could dismantle and sell off the buildings.

After a year, half the buildings were still standing. Bidding was opened to the public, and that's when the real action began. The Jupiter Island Club took several small buildings for mainte- nance sheds. The Baptist Congregation in Fort Pierce bought the camp chapel for $1,500 (where it stands today). The village of Hobe Sound got a large meeting hall for its civic center and if you should go by the Arthur Dehon Building in downtown Stuart, you'll see another Camp Murphy keepsake.

Perhaps the biggest beneficiary of the open bidding was Kurt Whiticar, then a young man in need of indoor space for his fledgling boatbuilding business in Stuart. Whiticar, in his nineties as this was written, had his eye on the camp's 70 x 90 foot cafeteria and snack bar. "I admired the strong 12-foot cypress rafters, but I didn't know how we'd break it [the building] up," he recalled. Whiticar put in a $475 bid and held his breath. No one else wanted the huge building. Whiticar solved his dismantling challenge by removing the roof and trusses, then taking down the sides in 8-foot sections and trucking everything off. Today the reconstructed building anchors the sprawling grounds of the successful Whiticar Boat Works Inc.

After the auctions, not much was left of Camp Murphy – and even less now. You can still see the top of a former water reservoir just east of the railroad tracks, but it's been sealed shut. The target wall of the rifle range still stands, and visitors continue to find spent shells in the hills beyond. Across from Hobe Mountain, a former barracks building is now home to a park ranger family.

Like a ghost of the past, a lone sentry box still stands guard along U.S. 1.

One of the most unusual remaining structures was built from one of three water reservoirs, each with walls and ceilings of thick poured concrete. The southernmost reservoir was covered with earth and turned into an underground civil defense headquarters as the Cold War heated up. Nicknamed the "cave," it contained emergency provisions for several federal and state officials: a self-contained water system, offices, sleeping areas with three tiers of cots, bathrooms, a laundry, a kitchen and several weeks' worth of military C-rations.

After the Civil Defense Office moved to a new site in the 1980s, the bunker served as headquarters for the state park staff until the new Elsa Kimball Research and Education Center was opened in 2007. Today the cave is still used as a storage facility.

No man's land

For three years after its decommissioning in 1944, the fate of this scarred, crisscrossed, pockmarked parcel of land remained in limbo. The federal government still owned the roughly 8,000 acres it had bought from the Reeds' Hobe Sound Company plus the bits and pieces confiscated from families like Dubois, but as the bureaucracy slowly ruminated on what to do with it, squatters returned. At one time or another parts were occupied by campers, hunters, vandals, and even a temporary, government-sponsored labor camp.

Developers showed up, too. One of them wanted a sizeable chunk of land along U.S. 1 to build "Holy Land," his dream of ersatz biblical theme park that would do for tiny Hobe Sound what Disney World did for Orlando. Well, a massive Noah's Ark wasn't what the Reed family wanted to see looming over the horizon from their tranquil Jupiter Island Club. It also aroused people like Edwin A. Menninger of Stuart. As he recalled in 1982, "I had been much involved in Camp Murphy because I owned and operated the Red Bus Line which hauled soldiers back and forth for three years – three million rides without an accident." While Menninger led a local effort to block speculators from grabbing any land, Mrs. Permelia Reed went straight to Governor Spessard Holland in a chartered plane.

By 1947 it was a foregone conclusion that the state of Florida would acquire the Camp Murphy land, and on June 9 the Florida Board of Forestry and Parks obtained title to 7,871 acres.

All it needed was a name before it officially became a state park. The tentative name

A lone barracks building stands today

was Jupiter State Park, but other minds were at work. At the time, John and Bessie Dubois were renting the original family home atop a shell mound near Jupiter Inlet to a retired Yale professor and his wife. In 1938 Professor Charles W. Andrews had stumbled on a musty, out-of-print book by Jonathan Dickinson about his harrowing escape from the Jeaga Indians in 1696. After seven years of research and editing, Andrews' version of the saga had been published in 1945 and suddenly the name of Jonathan Dickinson was again on the minds of local leaders. When state officials asked them if they had something better in mind than Jupiter State Park, Dickinson's name bubbled quickly to the surface.

With the deal done, did it mean that families like Dubois could now get back their confiscated land along beautiful Kitching Creek? When Bessie herself went to Tallahassee and asked, she was told that it would be impossible because it just wouldn't be the same state park without all those tall cypress along the creek – the very ones her John Dubois had saved by painting their trunks with white paint.

A park in name only

Jonathan Dickinson was now a state park, but merely saying so was a long way from being a properly restored, inviting attraction full of friendly rangers. The park district exercised at best passive dominion over the property while it waited in line for money in the state budget. Poachers hunted and boats sped upriver. Even the government itself contributed to the chaos by allowing a National Guard unit to spend weekends at the park shooting up the old target range and tearing up the scrubland with Jeeps and halftracks.

Moreover, the 1947 boundaries and 8,000 acres were too confined to allow park officials to properly protect the land and control its future. The state, for example, didn't own any land on the southern shore of the Loxahatchee, and this is why the person who held the key to its fate was none other than Vince "Trapper" Nelson.

By the mid-1960s Nelson had closed his Zoo and Jungle Garden to visitors by felling tree trunks across the river approaches to his dock. Now in his late fifties and with a midriff as massive as his chest, he had by then pieced together 857 acres of prime riverfront property and was anything but the free spirit who evoked a carefree Tarzan in his pristine jungle. Most of his time was consumed by fretting over high property taxes, fencing his domain off from squatters and guarding against hooligans and vandals. The rest of his time Trapper spent trying to sell his "ranch," as he called it — sometimes to developers by promising how much money they'd make by digging canals for waterfront homes, sometimes to nonprofit environmental groups by preaching on how they'd serve mankind by preserving the Loxahatchee.

Alice Delamar was a Palm Beach matron who owned a 40-acre weekend retreat on the river just east of Trapper's land. When she donated her land to the Audubon Society (which then assigned its management to the state park) she tried to act as a go-between in getting the Society to acquire her neighbor's land as well. But the deal invariably floundered on this or that condition imposed by Trapper (example: that he be allowed to continue hunting and trapping on the entire 857 acres).

After Delamar threw up her hands in despair, the state Bureau of Parks and Recreation gingerly approached the reclusive Trapper. In July 1968 the Bureau's delicate dickering had produced an initial agreement to pay him $1,500 an acre while letting him keep 100 acres around his camp for life. Vince Nelson would have been an instant millionaire. But then on July 30, his body was found face down on the earthen floor of his chickee hut with his spent shotgun at his side.

While police and coroners tried to determine the cause of his mysterious demise, Trapper's unguarded camp became open season for curiosity seekers, thieves and rowdy partiers. What's worse, his cabin and gardens were ransacked by vandals who'd heard rumors that the quirky recluse had buried cash all around the property.

Often it takes a scene so tragic that newspapers write exposés and people are shocked into action. In this case, the still-impoverished state park people were able to prevail on the Florida Game & Fresh Water Commission to post guards on the property. It also caught the eye of the developers of the upscale Lost Tree golfing community in North Palm Beach. They wanted to duplicate their success in

A park campsite in the 1950s

Jupiter-Tequesta and they made the state a proposition. If it would cede 360 acres of hilly scrub land along the southeast corner of U.S. 1, the developers would buy all of Trapper's 857 acres on the upper Loxahatchee and trade it for parkland even-up.

The desired land in Jonathan Dickinson happened to be little used. Fortuitously, it appraised at $1.3 million versus $1.33 million for Trapper's larger but less accessible tract. The deal spelled win-win-win all around. Vince Nelson's heirs in far-off Trenton, N.J. stood to become overnight millionaires. The developers turned the scrubby hills into the lush fairways that would become the Jupiter Hills Club, one of the nation's top-ranked golf courses. The park gained its long-sought stretch along the south shore of the Loxahatchee and its biggest visitor attraction to boot.

The park's second lucky break came in 1981 when governor Bob Graham prevailed on the Florida legislature to pass the Save Our Rivers Act. In general, the new law levied a surcharge on all documentary stamps issued in real estate transactions. The extra funds would be parceled out to the state's regional water management districts, which would then purchase lands along environmentally-sensitive rivers.

The acquisitions money allowed Jonathan Dickinson planners to focus on a patchwork of family-owned plots along the curvy ribbon that formed the upper Loxahatchee. Located mostly between Indiantown Road and the park's Trapper Nelson tract, the acreage follows the south-to-north current of the river beneath a jungle-like canopy of cypress and fern before it swings east and widens. Located within this roughly two-mile stretch were old orange groves, truck farms and unimproved pasture that had been settled by Palm Beach families since the turn of the 20th century. Some had put up their own dams to divert water for farming. One had built a crude bridge so he could haul crops across the river. One owner had sold to an RV park developer who put in dozens of concrete slabs and barbecue pits.

Save Our Rivers saved the upper Loxahatchee by acquiring 1,461 acres from area landowners. Just one example is the 18-acre Lainhart tract, owned since the 1890s as a grove and weekend retreat by one of Palm Beach's pioneer families. By the 1980s the cabins and cook shed on the property were falling prey to old age, vandals and weekend partiers. A crude dam that the Lainharts had erected to help irrigate their crops was beginning to fall apart. The family was happy to have the South Florida Water Management District (SFWMD) acquire the 18 acres with Save Our Rivers money. The District rebuilt the dam to help regulate the flow of fresh water downstream and installed a "ladder" at one end so that paddlers could portage their canoes and kayaks. Today, one of the restored Lainhart cottages is used to house a park staff member.

The third and final piece of the land puzzle was supplied by an unlikely benefactor. In the 1960s just about everyone in South Florida knew that its largest landowner was John D. MacArthur with more than 100,000 acres. MacArthur was also known as its biggest eccentric. Years before he had acquired the nearly-bankrupt Bankers Life and Casualty Co. and parlayed it into a billion dollar fortune by selling cheap burial policies to working people door to door. Now he ruled his empire from a table in the coffee shop of a dowdy oceanfront hotel that he owned in Palm Beach Shores.

One of MacArthur's favorite pursuits was acquiring even more land, and his agents nibbled constantly at the upper

Trapper's bedroom ransacked at the height of the vandalism after his death.

Loxahatchee in search of tracts that could be laced with canals for waterfront developments. Sometimes it meant skirmishing with Trapper Nelson. Twice MacArthur brought the eager Trapper to the brink of selling his ranch, only to wave Banker's Life stock in his face instead of cash. To Trapper, stock was just another form of swindle, and he'd stalk off cursing all developers and lawyers.

Well, just as it took Trapper Nelson's death to pry loose his land, it was the crusty tycoon's death in 1978 that triggered creation of the John D. and Catherine T. MacArthur Foundation. One of its chief objectives was to sell or manage 100,000 acres in the heart of bustling, booming South Florida. In 1985 the Foundation donated 903 acres to the park and it was matched by a similar gift from the Nature Conservancy. With the other odds and ends acquired from smaller landowners, Jonathan Dickinson State Park now encompassed today's approximately 11,500 acres.

All this was happening while another movement was gaining speed on a separate track. So many developers were hacking away at the edges of the river and park that local folks were beginning to conclude that only the might of the federal government could stop it. In one case during 1965, wily John D. MacArthur had quietly obtained a permit to build canals just east of the park and locals didn't even find out until they looked out over the river one day and saw a giant dredge at work scouring out oyster beds to a depth of 12 feet.

Even government agencies were raising eyebrows. Four miles upriver, the state Department of Transportation was bringing Interstate 95 northward and wanted it to slice smack through the park at Trapper Nelson's place. Then in 1980 the Army Corps of Engineers unveiled a plan to alleviate the dirty stormwater surges rushing down the St. Lucie Canal from Lake Okeechobee. The proposed "solution" was to link the St. Lucie Canal to the Loxahatchee via a 300-foot wide, 30-foot deep canal.

In 1977 the Jupiter-Tequesta Women's Club began advocating that some entity with more muscle than a couple of small towns be brought to bear on the matter. Ten years earlier Congress had enacted the Wild and Scenic Rivers Act, and even though none had been designated for preservation in Florida, obtaining this status for the Loxahatchee gradually became the common objective of local leaders in Jupiter-Tequesta and the Florida Park Service. By 1985, after a comprehensive study by several government agencies, the National Park Service determined that the portion of the Loxahatchee within the state park was eligible to become a Wild and Scenic River. Later that year Congress made it official.

The Loxahatchee watershed

Maybe the most important thing about the park for a visitor to grasp is that its 11,500 acres are only a piece of the 240-square-mile watershed that drains into the Loxahatchee River. And if the river had to depend on just the freshwater within its own boundaries, sea water might soon be rushing in from Jupiter Inlet to fill the void and changing the cypress environment to mangroves.

For example, during the 1960s and 70s, some dredging projects were undertaken around Jupiter Inlet that made it easier for more seawater to rush upriver. Around the same time, much of the natural headwaters flow was being diminished by a recently-dug canal (C-18) that channeled water into the river's South Fork. To keep the upper (western) reaches of the Loxahatchee from being parched, a gated structure (G-92) was built to divert some of the flow from the C-18 canal. Overall, it gave the system the capacity to increase the flow of fresh water far upstream.

These man-made partial solutions only helped planners realize the importance of bringing as much of the natural watershed drainage system under public control as possible. Recently what are perhaps the best long-term benefits to

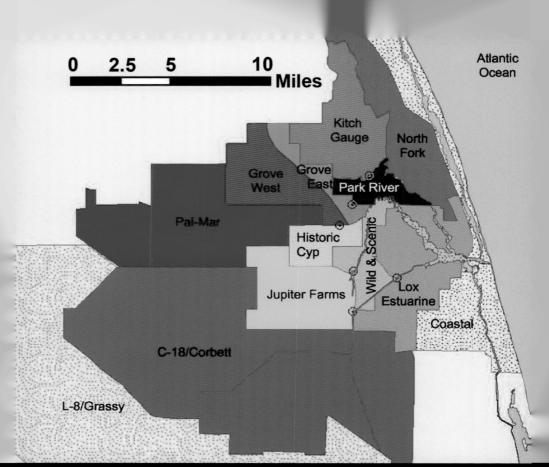

The 240 square mile Loxahatchee watershed cosists of 12 drainage systems, as shown above.

Jonathan Dickinson State Park have taken place just outside its boundaries. During the decade that began in 1996 some major acquisitions were made under the Florida Forever program and various bond issues. As a result:

- The 16,000-acre Atlantic Ridge, which touches on JDSP's northwest border, has been earmarked for purchase from its private owners. Besides providing connectivity with wildlife, it represents one of the best remaining patches of scrub, pine flatwoods and marshes.

- Much of the 35,600-acre Pal-Mar area, making up a large chunk of the Loxahatchee's western watershed, has already been purchased, using a mix of county, SFWMD and Florida Forever funds. Its wet prairie is the "sponge" that retains and filters water before it enters the river.

- Cypress Creek and its surrounding wetlands are being acquired, preserved, and restored. Prior to the restoration, studies showed that this tributary, which enters the Loxahatchee just north of the Trapper Nelson site, carried a high degree of suspended sediments — mostly from agricultural drainage.

- Riverbend Park, owned by Palm Beach County, opened in 2007 after an extensive restoration that followed acquisition of its 680 acres in 1992. In a way, Riverbend is a continuation of the state park because it contains the portion of the Loxahatchee on the south side of Indiantown Road.

Other land acquisitions are in the works in the watershed, affording the Loxahatchee a fighting chance to remain a truly "wild and scenic" river. But other challenges remain, as explained in chapter four.

The Loxahachee River: mile by mile

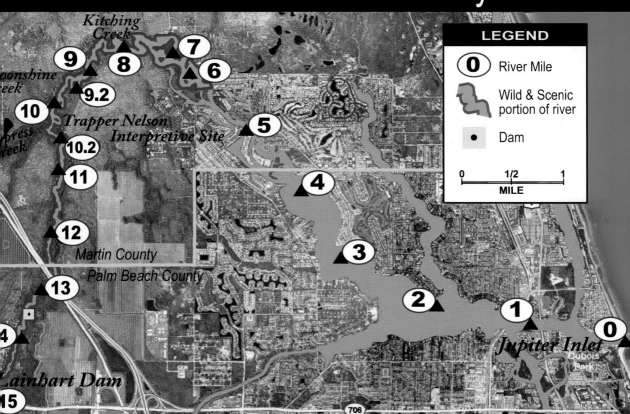

The big picture

The Florida we walk on has a sandy surface underlain by limestone. But not originally. The "basement" of the Florida Plateau, which runs north-south between the deep basins of the Atlantic Ocean and Gulf of Mexico, actually consists of volcanic rocks produced by upheavals millions of years ago. What's now on the surface is the result of seawater covering the land — then receding — in a cycle that took thousands of years.

When the sea covered the Florida Plateau it left deposits of sediments. When it withdrew, most of the sediment stayed behind. In time the sedimentary deposits caked and hardened into a level blanket of limestone lying nearly two miles thick over the volcanic bedrock in the "basement."

Roughly 100,000 years ago marked the beginning of the three cycles that made up the most recent, or Wisconsin Ice Age. Each cycle resulted in South Florida disappearing underwater except for the tops of some sand hills. It's the limestone deposits from these cycles that today form the gravely, muddy "marl" that nourishes our plants and trees.

The three wet-dry cycles that began 100,000 years ago left the park's eastern portion with sandbars and dunes on its higher terraces. The tall sand dunes became barrier islands and formed the backbone of the Atlantic Coastal Ridge that included Hobe Mountain and the tall dune on which Jupiter's lighthouse was built.

As the glaciers of the Wisconsin Ice Age advanced, the water level in the ocean dropped because it no longer received water from rivers. Around 20,000 years ago, the sea reached a low point of some 300 feet below today's level. The climate was windy, cool and dry, leading to formation of large sand dunes.

Then from about 15,000 to 6,000 years ago the glaciers began to melt up north. As a result, the Atlantic Ocean rose at the rate of more than three feet per century. Near the end of this period the rise in sea level slowed and today's climate-vegetation became established. As the sea continued to rise, the fresh water Loxahatchee River/Indian River estuary became influenced by the intrusion of salt water.

The geological formations underlying the area form two aquifers separated by thick beds of limestone that kept them apart. In the upper strata was (is) a shallow surfical aquifer of permeable sand, limestone and shell beds running 15 to 150 feet deep, which is today the main source of fresh water for pubic utilities. Below that, ranging from 600 to 1,500 feet deep, was the Floridian or artesian aquifer, made up of marl, clay and more mineralized water.

Today, the South Florida land mass isn't perfectly flat. Looking from north to south, a cross-section would resemble a very shallow, slightly tilted saucer. Lake Okeechobee is a sort of saucer itself, sitting about 21 feet above sea level with a slight tilt to the south and west. This explains why almost all of the rivers and man-made canals leading from the lake rely on gravity as they drain slowly into the Gulf, the Atlantic Ocean or into Florida Bay at the southern tip.

Of all those inland waterways in South Florida, only the Loxahatchee River operates apart from Lake Okeechobee and its gravity system. Its water supply comes chiefly from its 240-square-mile drainage basin of rain and wetlands. And it's why, when new homes and golf courses suck water from that basin and lower the water table, they risk imperiling the flow to Florida's first Wild and Scenic River.

Like most drainage basins in South Florida, the Loxahatchee has a rich diversity of plant communities. The flatness of the terrain means that sites varying only a few inches in height can give rise to markedly different plant communities and wildlife.

South Florida's climate is also favorable for many plants and animals of the Caribbean tropics. Despite all those sea level changes over the centuries, it has never had a land connection to the West Indies. However, birds, hurricanes and the Gulf Stream have all brought an abundance of seeds from the Caribbean. Long before man arrived on the scene, South Florida was a mixed assortment of tropical West Indian species and northern continental species.

Now stir in an influx of farm animals, agricultural crops and hitch-hiking insects brought by "colonists" ranging from Spanish explorers to modern vacationers and you can begin to understand why South Florida has one of the most varied arrays of flora in the world.

Within that impressive diversity stands Jonathan Dickinson State Park. JDSP's 11,500 acres host 147 recorded plant families, of which 130 are flowering. By comparison, Everglades National Park, with its 1.5 million acres, supports 152 plant families.

Now, let's begin to identify and steer you towards these "vegetation communities" as you set out on the park's trails. Although biologists have actually identified 15 separate communities, or ecosystems, we'll focus here on just the eight most prevalent.

The *Shrinking scrub*

Sand Pine

Myrtle Oak

Sand Live Oak

One of Florida's oldest natural communities, scrub is generally formed on sand ridges along ancient shorelines and now appears as a sparse forest of sand pines with an understory of oaks and saw palmetto growing in quickly-drained, sterile, brilliant white sand. Its plants have adapted to the dry conditions by growing extensive root systems and thick, leathery leaves to retain moisture.

In JDSP you'll find 2,310 acres of scrub, mostly along the eastern boundary capped by the 86-foot dune, Hobe Mountain. The low, stunted landscape takes up some 20 percent of the entire park and is one of the largest remaining stretches of scrub land in South Florida. An estimated 95 percent of South Florida's original scrubland has disappeared, beginning with pineapple growers a hundred years ago and then accelerated by the explosion of residential development along the coast. Scrub especially appeals to developers because it's on high, dry land can be cleared more easily than thick forests. Indeed, it's one of the reasons that the military builders of Camp Murphy were able to erect 600 buildings and a maze of roads in just a few months.

Even more recently, scrub has been further endangered by the invasion of all-terrain vehicles, which tear up the delicate groundcover and hasten the erosion of sand. Damaged ground lichens can take up to 50 years to recover.

CHAPTER TWO: *The Shrinking Scrub*

What remains is a fascinating landscape full of hardy survivors. The trees tend to be short and gnarly. The most visible is the **sand pine,** often with twisted trunks and branches. It has brown, smooth bark with cones and needles each about four inches long.

Also prevalent are the **sand live oak,** with long, oval green leaves, and the **myrtle oak,** with more rounded leaves. Alongside the **sand pines, scrub oaks and myrtle oaks** are such residents as:

SAW PALMETTO, named for the saw-like teeth along its stalks. This slow-growing palm produces dark brown berries that were once a dietary staple for early Indians. Today the berries are grown commercially for their claimed ability to retard growth of the male prostate gland.

PRICKLY PEAR CACTUS, the "porcupine" of the plant world. It appears in several dry communities and its bright yellow flowers appear in early summer. The cactus is fed upon by the cochineal scale beetle, which South American Indians collected and mashed to produce a red dye coveted by Spanish royalty. Early settlers in South Florida learned that if they peeled back the spiny cactus "pad," the fruity pulp inside could be sliced for salads, added to drinks for a tasty tang and used as a thickener in soups and stews.

ROSEMARY, an aromatic, large-flowered shrub, not to be confused with the herb used for cooking. A member of the mint family, rosemary has tiny leaves that curl so tightly to conserve water that they resemble needles.

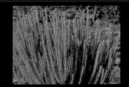

SCRUB MINT, which prefers sunny, open areas. When in bloom it has a pale, bluish-purple flower with a remarkably minty odor.

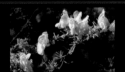

GREENBRIER, with its thorny vines resembling barbed wire. You'd never think that its roots and leaves were frequent food for Native Americans.

The small, delicate **DANCING LADY,** usually found within leaf litter or near the lower branches of the Florida rosemary shrub or scrub plants. It's unique only to the eastern scrub communities of Martin and Palm Beach counties.

The **FOUR-PETALLED PAWPAW**, with its spring-blooming white blossoms and waxy, leathery leaves to conserve water. It's a very rare, endangered species found only in few parts of Martin County.

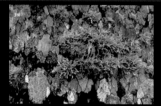

LICHENS, which spread across open areas with a wooly or sponge-like growth. A lichen is made up of microscopic strands of fungus and the cells of algae. The food produced by the algae is shared with the fungus, which furnishes moisture and nutrients for the algae

Florida Scrub-jay

Scurrying in and about this intricate ground cover are a bewildering array of animals and insects, all competing for berries, blooms and roots. Animals you'll most likely spot on the trail: the **Florida scrub-lizard, red widow spider, eastern coachwhip snake, eastern indigo snake, southern black racer, the spotted skunk** and rare **Florida mouse.**

When it comes to birds, don't forget to look down as well as up! Some species depend on a supply of seeds and berries that have dropped to the ground. You'll be especially lucky if you spot the threatened **Florida scrub-jay**. This species depends on insects and vegetation found in the open scrub, and keeping the scrub low in height depends on periodic prescribed fires. It's an important part of park management, and is detailed in chapter four.

Spotted Skunk

Florida Scrub-lizard

Red Widow Spider

Although they're common in north Florida, Jonathan Dickinson State Park is the farthest southeast you'll see sandhills. They appear in three areas near the southern border. The first is just west of the Pine Grove Campground near U.S. Highway 1. The second is on the north bank of the Loxahatchee in the River Campground area. The third is on the Trapper Nelson property. These areas combined cover 141 acres.

Sandhills, occurring on hilltops and the slopes of gently rolling hills, are composed of deep, marine-deposited, yellowish sands that are well drained and relatively sterile. They spawn a widely spaced forest primarily of slash pines and turkey oak.

Slash pines have a widespread root system, which is why you may see them bent back from the prevailing southeast wind. These evergreens, with clusters of long needles reaching to a foot each, can grow to 60 feet and live up to 200 years. Inside their plate-like bark is hard wood used for poles and railroad ties. They've also been tapped over the centuries for turpentine and rosin.

You can recognize **turkey oaks** by their wispy green leaves and large acorns. They get their name from three-lobed leaves that resemble a turkey's foot. Growing 20 to 30 feet high, their wood is heavy, hard and reddish brown. It's been used widely for lumber and fuel. The acorns are staples for a wide range of park animals.

Turkey Oak

Slash Pine

The sandhills have a fairly dense cover of grasses and herbs. Among them are such interesting mainstays as:

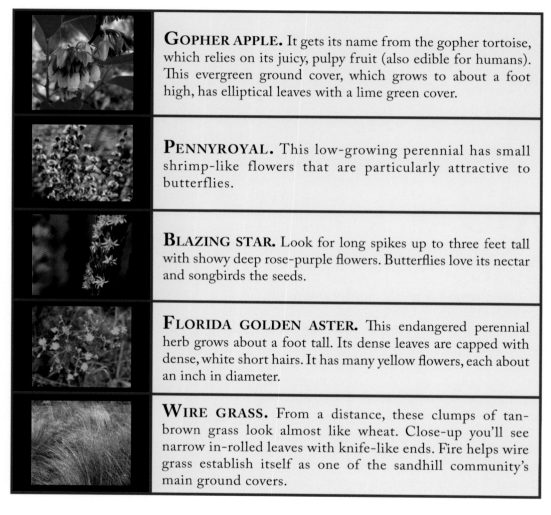

GOPHER APPLE. It gets its name from the gopher tortoise, which relies on its juicy, pulpy fruit (also edible for humans). This evergreen ground cover, which grows to about a foot high, has elliptical leaves with a lime green cover.

PENNYROYAL. This low-growing perennial has small shrimp-like flowers that are particularly attractive to butterflies.

BLAZING STAR. Look for long spikes up to three feet tall with showy deep rose-purple flowers. Butterflies love its nectar and songbirds the seeds.

FLORIDA GOLDEN ASTER. This endangered perennial herb grows about a foot tall. Its dense leaves are capped with dense, white short hairs. It has many yellow flowers, each about an inch in diameter.

WIRE GRASS. From a distance, these clumps of tan-brown grass look almost like wheat. Close-up you'll see narrow in-rolled leaves with knife-like ends. Fire helps wire grass establish itself as one of the sandhill community's main ground covers.

Typical animals in the sandhills are the **barking treefrog, gopher frog, gopher tortoise, Florida pine snake, eastern diamondback rattlesnake** and **Florida scarlet snake.**

JDSP is especially known for its many **gopher tortoises.** The typical tortoise is ten inches long, weighs nine pounds and lives 40 – 60 years in the wild. That is, they did until the age of highways, which is why they are now a "Species of Special Concern" in Florida.

Eastern Diamondback Rattler

The gopher tortoise depends on low-growing grasses and herbs, which means having an open canopy overhead so that sunlight can nourish groundcover. Equally important are sandy soils for digging burrows. In a typical year a gopher tortoise will dig 17 burrows, each around 15 feet long and six feet deep. He's known as the "landlord" of the park because so many frogs, turtles and snakes depend on him for their homes.

Gopher Tortoise

If you're a birdwatcher, look for **bobwhite, ground dove** and **rufous-sided towhee.**

Sandhills are important areas for filtering water down to the aquifers because the porous sands allow it to move rapidly through them with little runoff and minimal evaporation.

The deep sandy soils create a xeric environment that is aided by the ample, scattered spacing between trees. This allows more sunlight to warm the ground during the day and cool it more rapidly at night. Thus, temperature and humidity fluctuations are generally greater in Sandhills than in nearby closed canopy forests.

Bobwhite

Fire plays a big role in maintaining the ecology of this community. Frequent fires reduce competition among hardwoods and enhance growth of grasses. For more on the dramatic role of prescribed burns in the park, see chapter four, page **78.**

Rufous-sided towhee

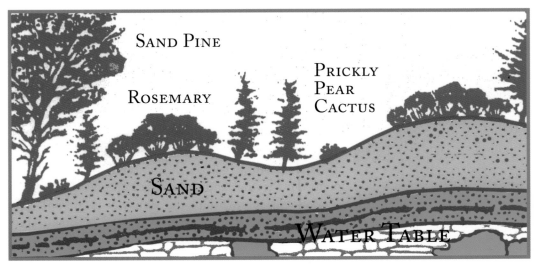

Cross section of a typical sandhill area

Wet flatwoods: a hiker's heaven

Shiny Blueberry

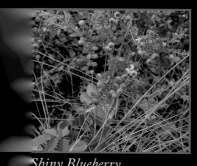

White-tailed deer

With some 4,900 acres, these relatively open-canopy forests of scattered **slash pines, wax myrtle, saw palmetto** and **shiny blueberry** comprise nearly half of the park's surface. Most of this community is found west of the railroad tracks and on the paved one mile biking-hiking trail. But much of it also lies well beyond, in the primitive northwest portion of the park that is designated as a State Wilderness Preserve.

Biologists today debate whether the flatwoods are truly "subtropical." For example, if you see a raccoon, blue jay or black snake as you walk through the park, you might say "There's nothing subtropical about these. I can see them in Illinois or Ohio." However, the tree climbed by the raccoon, the insect caught by the blue jay and the lizard just eaten by the black snake are likely to be subtropical species not found up north.

Wet flatwoods (mixed with some mesic, or sparsely canopied flatwoods) invariably grow on flat, poorly drained terrain. The soils typically consist of one to three feet of acidic sands overlying an organic hardpan or clay layer. The hardpan restricts water from percolating beneath it, which is why you'll often see water standing on the surface during the rainy season. Then during the cool and dry season, ground water is less accessible for many plants whose roots haven't been able to work their way through the hardpan. Thus, many plants are stressed by water saturation during the wet seasons and stressed by dehydration during dry stretches.

Besides the ever-present saw palmetto, some of the more interesting shrubs and ground cover you'll see in the wet flatwoods include:

DEER TONGUE, so named because of its long and narrow leaves. They smell of vanilla, and were ground into a tea by early settlers to help reduce fever.

GALLBERRY, a prolific evergreen with reddish twigs and purple berries. Its leaves have been used to make tea.

LOPSIDED INDIAN GRASS, a perennial native bunchgrass that typically grows three to four feet in the flatwoods (look for it on the Kitching Creek Trail). Each plant produces a purple tuft with golden brown panicles of grain-like seeds that become diet staples from birds to cattle in south Florida.

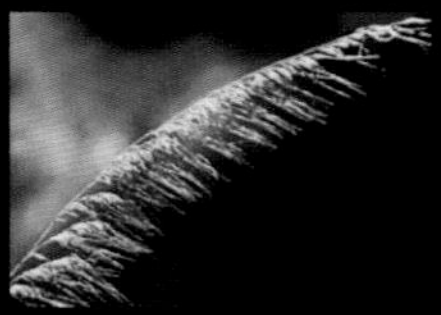

TARFLOWER, a woody shrub with fragrant, showy white-pink flowers that can grow over six feet tall. Its nectar is coveted by butterflies and its sticky flowers trap flies and other insects.

GRASS-PINK (calopogon species). One of the most common wild orchids in South Florida, it grows from ten to 30 inches tall and produces beautiful, slender flowers of white to deep pink.

SENSITIVE BRIER, a groundcover with long, narrow green leaves and a pink flower. It's spiny and armored with hooked prickles.

BACHELOR'S BUTTON, a hardy annual that produces small, round flower with many rays bursting around a "button" in the center.

STAGGERBUSH, a perennial shrub with ribbed, brown limbs that grows to about five feet. Its leaves are elliptical with a rough, pale back side.

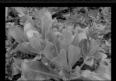

BEACHBERRY, a sprawling shrub, now on Florida's endangered plant list, with green leaves and a black-blue berry that produces a white flower.

Florida Bobcat

When the pine flatwoods have a thick shrubby understory, you'll see only a sparse ground cover. Or if the understory is skimpy you can expect a dense ground cover of hydrophytic (water-friendly) herbs and shrubs.

Besides the usual cast of characters **(bobcat, raccoon and opossum)**, the flatwoods' animal population includes **white-tailed deer, cottontail rabbit, cotton rat, cotton mouse, corn snake, dusky pygmy rattlesnake, eastern garter snake, coral snake, oak toad, cricket frog** and **chorus frog**. You may also see **feral hogs**, much to the chagrin of park rangers. As the wild pigs root about the soft, moist soil with their snouts, these intruders cause serious erosion to the park.

Raccoon

Coral Snake

Among birds, the more open ground is preferred by the **red shouldered hawk** to spot prey from on high. **Bobwhite, meadowlark** and **great-crested flycatcher** also thrive where there is open canopy, but they may be hard to spot in areas where underbrush is not controlled by fire.

Covering roughly 870 acres in the central and western sections of the park, this poorly drained, marshy prairie is a treeless wetland. It has a sparse to dense groundcover of grasses and herbs in a sandy soil. It's usually adjacent to the flatwoods and grades into them. Within the park the wet prairie serves as part of the filtering system for the Loxahatchee River. And because it retains water in times of drought, it helps reduce the impact of salt moving upriver in those times.

Wet prairies are becoming rarer in south Florida because of damage by off-road vehicles, a long-term lowering of the groundwater table and a host of species that want to move into the neighborhood. **Melaleuca**, **slash pines** and **wax myrtle** are examples of trees that love sucking up excessive amounts of water at the expense of everything else around them. And, again, it's why periodic prescribed fires are required to keep intruders at bay.

The ground cover, which also benefits from fire, includes:

Melaleuca Tree

TOOTHACHE GRASS. Growing to four feet tall, the stalks are dark green with a paler green on the underside. It produces arched, beige spikettes that can measure up to six inches each.

MAIDENCANE. A semi-erect grass that grows to 40 inches tall and produces an elongated panicle (tuft) of six to eight inches at the end of a lush green leaf. It spreads via *rhizomes*, horizontal, root-like stems that send out roots from their lower surfaces and shoots from the upper part.

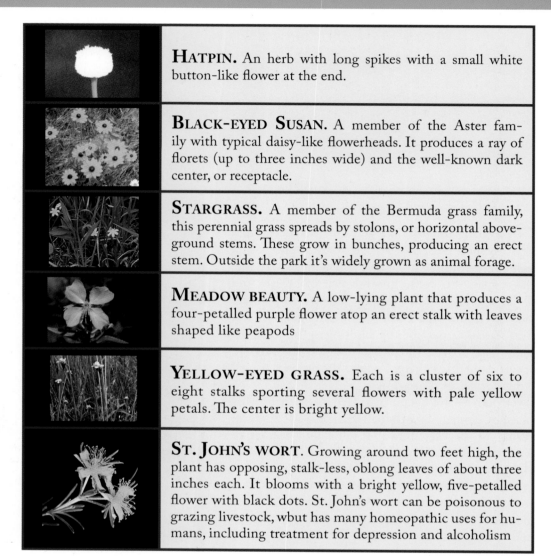

HATPIN. An herb with long spikes with a small white button-like flower at the end.

BLACK-EYED SUSAN. A member of the Aster family with typical daisy-like flowerheads. It produces a ray of florets (up to three inches wide) and the well-known dark center, or receptacle.

STARGRASS. A member of the Bermuda grass family, this perennial grass spreads by stolons, or horizontal above-ground stems. These grow in bunches, producing an erect stem. Outside the park it's widely grown as animal forage.

MEADOW BEAUTY. A low-lying plant that produces a four-petalled purple flower atop an erect stalk with leaves shaped like peapods

YELLOW-EYED GRASS. Each is a cluster of six to eight stalks sporting several flowers with pale yellow petals. The center is bright yellow.

ST. JOHN'S WORT. Growing around two feet high, the plant has opposing, stalk-less, oblong leaves of about three inches each. It blooms with a bright yellow, five-petalled flower with black dots. St. John's wort can be poisonous to grazing livestock, wbut has many homeopathic uses for humans, including treatment for depression and alcoholism

Larger animals and snakes tend to be the same as in the neighboring wet flatlands. As for birds, the wet prairie attracts such species as **southeastern kestrel, killdeer, long-billed marsh wren, red-winged blackbird** and that handsome hawk, the **northern harrier.**

Northern Harrier

Red Winged Backbird

Meet the cleanup crew

Turkey Vultures

Although you may have come to the park to see the osprey and eagle, you're more likely to see a whole lot more of the **turkey vulture.** They perch in clusters, usually along the riverfront, and they unnerve a lot of folks because they just sit there staring silently.

The turkey vulture's plumage is dark brown. It weighs about six pounds and has a wingspan of up to six feet. Once it takes flight and begins gliding on an air pocket, few birds are more graceful.

No, its red, bald head wouldn't get many votes in a beauty pageant, but there's a practical reason. When the vulture is eating carrion, it must often stick its head inside the carcass to reach the meat. A feathery head would capture unwanted pieces of the vulture's meal, along with all the bacteria it hosts.

The turkey vulture also has a good excuse for its infernal silence. Its vocalization capabilities are limited to uttering weak hisses (when threatened) and grunts (during courtship).

By the way, turkey vultures don't feed solely on carrion. When lacking success in finding their favorite food, they will dine on all sorts of shoreline vegetation and even some farm crops

Killdeer

Chances are that sometime during your visit you'll hear the loud clatter of a **sandhill crane** family flying overhead. If so, these tall cranes, which grow to three feet with a six-foot wingspan, are probably heading for home somewhere in the wet prairie.

Sandhill Crane

Florida's forest primeval: the cypress dome

Pond Cypress

Southern Cricket Frog

If you took the horseback trail beyond the wet flatwoods to the park's northwest sector, you'd see an unusual 26 acres: stands or clumps of mostly cypress, each with a canopy resembling a sculptured dome. But you can also see a small one about half way up the main park road on your way to the River Campground. It's off to the left opposite the EaglesView Multi-Use Trail.

The typical cypress dome grows in sandy flatwoods where sand has slumped around or over a sinkhole, creating a conical depression. The "dome" gets its shape because bigger trees grow in deeper water at the center while the younger ones grow in the shallower waters at the outer edge. The soil in the center is thick with peat that stays wet or moist year-around.

Dome swamps get much of their water through runoff from surrounding uplands, or may be connected with underground channels. They may function as reservoirs that recharge the aquifer when adjacent water tables drop during drought periods.

The trees you'll find most common in the park's domed swamps are **pond cypress**, **red maple** (which can grow to 50 feet), and **slash pine**. You may also see **dahoon holly**, **swamp bay**, **loblolly bay**, and **pond apple**.

Spanish Moss   *Chain Fern*   *Swamp Bay*   *Loblolly Bay*

Prevalent plants and bushes include **Virginia willow, fetterbush, chain fern, poison ivy, laurel greenbrier, Spanish moss, wild pine, royal fern, coastal plain willow, loblolly bay, orchids, buttonbush, fire flag, and shoestring fern.**

The animals who like living under the dome include the **southern cricket frog, mud turtle.**

Also look for these birds on your visit: **wood stork, wood duck, swallow-tailed kite, pileated woodpecker, great-crested flycatcher, prothonotory warbler** and **rusty blackbird.**

A big reason why these swamps keep that domed shape is fire maintenance. Without periodic fires – usually every three to five years on the periphery – the community would be invaded by hardwoods. Peat would accumulate and change the swamp to a bottomland forest or bog. Light, managed fire also helps keep the peat soil moist without harming the cypress. If the peat were allowed to dry out and catch fire by natural causes, the dome would soon become a treeless pond.

Pileated Woodpecker   *Wood Stork*   *Wood Duck*   *Swallow Tailed Kite*

Strand swamp: making creeks distinctive

Otter

Royal Fern

I n its textbook form, a strand swamp is a forest, dominated by bald cypress, that stands in an elongated trough of a flat limestone plain. Somewhat like the domed swamp, strand swamps have a rounded look from afar because younger trees stand on the outer edges, grading into large older ones in the interior. Trees in the top canopy are mainly temperate, while understory and air (epiphytic) plants tend to be tropical. The soil is peat and sand over limestone.

In Jonathan Dickinson those "elongated troughs" form the creeks that feed the Loxahatchee. Although they cover around 916 acres in all, their make-up can vary from creek to creek due to different rates of water flow and the fact that some streams are feeling the effects of ditches and canals created by farmers in their headwaters beyond the park borders.

When someone digs a ditch upstream, it tends to speed the rate of flow into the Loxahatchee, bringing sediment and pollutants into the river that were once filtered out by plants and sand. For example, most of Kitching Creek's natural channel lies within the park boundaries, so its flow is more apt to follow its traditional pattern. But up around mile marker nine near Trapper Nelson's camp, Moonshine Creek and Hobe Grove Canal have only part of their natural channel within the park. Growers have dammed and ditched much of the upper waterways, giving the Loxahatchee a major silt and sediment problem when summer rains bring heavy runoff.

If you walk the Kitching Creek Trail, you can pick out the major trees in a typical strand swamp along the water. Among the most prevalent:

BALD CYPRESS, a deciduous conifer, losing its needles by the end of November and leafing out again in March. Seedlings of bald cypress can't survive when soils are permanently flooded. But when mature, bald cypress is among the most flood tolerant of all tree species in Florida. Bald cypress can reach formidable heights and ages – some 165 feet tall and a few centuries old – making them among the most valuable attractions in the park.

CABBAGE PALM, the official state tree of Florida, is an evergreen with a fibrous trunk that can grow 80 feet into the canopy. Its four-to-five-foot long leaves are like large blades. Its berries resemble acorns, but hang in great clusters.

LAUREL OAK, a canopy tree that attains heights of 40-50 feet. Its seeds are eaten and disbursed by wildlife.

RED MAPLE, a water-loving deciduous tree that can grow to heights of 40-50 feet. The leaves are 4 to 6 inches long with red stems and serrated edges and red stems. In the fall they turn red and yellow, just like their cousins in New England.

POND APPLE is mostly a sub-canopy species, often stout with a buttressed trunk that can attain heights of 20 feet. Like cabbage palm, it grows best along streams and ponds. Pond apple seeds are distributed by flowing water, which reach many wildlife.

Forming the underbrush are **myrsine, buttonbush, poison ivy, swamp lily, leather fern** and **royal fern.**

In bygone years, **black bears** and **panthers** frequented the strand swamp. Today both are scarce here. You're more apt to **see raccoon, otter, white-tailed deer, opossum, gray squirrel, eastern mud snake,** and **striped crayfish snake.**

Floodplain swamp: the Loxahatchee's 'artery'

Turtle

Florida Cottonmouth (water moccasin)

Floodplain swamp is simply the name for the ribbon of mostly-saturated vegetation that lines the upper fresh water Loxahatchee River and its oxbows. The entire narrow shoreline, which begins around River Mile 8, takes up some 290 acres.

Except for several dry weeks in the winter, the soil on the riverbanks is under water either always or at least during a day's two high tides. Soils are a highly variable mixtures of sand, alluvial sediment and organic material such as decayed leaves and bark. This rich organic debris gives the river its "tea" color and helps provide nutrients to estuaries far downstream.

The primary shoreline trees are **bald cypress, pop ash, red maple** and **water hickory**.

The understory tends to be sparse, with such plants as **cocoplum, wild coffee,** and **royal fern.**

Among animals, riverbanks are the favorite haunt of the famous **Florida alligator.** Recent surveys estimate the park's gator population at around 60. In summer, when heavy run-off of water down the Loxahatchee freshens the brackish streams and bays, alligators move further down into the park. During these times of high water they may appear almost anywhere, even in shallow ditches off the roads. But in the dryer winter and spring, gators begin to seek the deeper ponds and sloughs. In fact, they often play a role as hydraulic engineers, much as beavers do in mountain streams. Big alligators dig ponds in low places and return to these private retreats each dry season, deepening and enlarging the pond as the years pass.

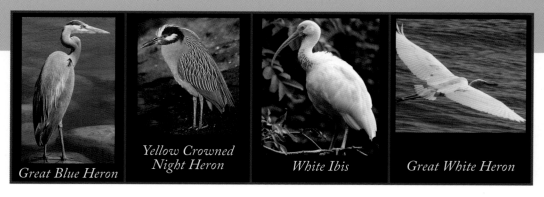

Great Blue Heron

*Yellow Crowned
Night Heron*

White Ibis

Great White Heron

An alligator dines on fish, turtles and any bird or small mammal careless enough to stray too close. Mating occurs in April and May. The female builds a nest of mud and rotting vegetation, sculpts a muddy alcove for her eggs, then guards the spot until the eggs hatch -- usually in late summer or early fall. Hatchling gators average about ten inches long. They grow at the rate of about a foot a year for the first few years, and then more slowly as they become an adult in around ten years. In our park an adult is typically eight to ten feet long, but some of 12 and 13 feet have been cited occasionally.

Next in the animal hierarchy (by size) in the floodplain swamp are the **bobcat, otter, raccoon, opossum** and **wood rat.** Then comes several species of **skink** and **frog** as well as the **Florida cottonmouth, black swamp snake** and **banded water snake.**

Surveying all this by air are the waterfowl that depend on what lives in and around the river. At the top of the pecking order is the **bald eagle,** of which there may be only one or two nesting pairs in the park at any one time. If you see a large, treetop nest (usually a dead cypress), it probably belongs to an **osprey** and his mate, who dive for fresh fish and squeal with delight as they carry their catch in their talons to the young ones in their nest.

Also perched high above, but probably on the look for small land-based prey is the **red shouldered hawk** and **barred owl.** Hunting along the shore on foot you're apt to see the **great blue heron, white ibis, yellow-crowned night heron and great white heron**.

In the stretch of river from the park concession area to Trapper Nelson's (roughly mile marker 6 to mile 9.5) the movement of the saltwater wedge up the Loxahatchee River from Jupiter Inlet has caused the floodplain swamp to change from a freshwater, cypress-dominated habitat to one that is now largely red and white mangroves The freshwater communities remain threatened by a drop in the general water table and by reduced water input to the river caused by urban development near the headwaters and along the tributaries. The spread of exotic Old World climbing fern also poses a very severe threat to this community.

Two kayakers in Kitching Creek had the presence of mind to photograph this 12-foot gator catching some rays as they slid by just a few feet away

Show me the blooms!

Spanish Moss

Park visitors are sometimes disappointed at not finding a profusion of showy wild flowers. One reason is that most folks arrive during the dry winter. While Florida plants don't go through the usual dormant period imposed by cold weather up north, many of them do enter a sort of resting stage when they produce fewer flowers than in other seasons.

Another factor holding down the number of flowering plants is that thick forest canopies shade the groundcover below most of the time. And along the river the ground may be flooded for long periods or consist of saline soils.

This is why **vines** and **air plants** are a prominent feature of forest vegetation. They represent a diverse selection of species with all sorts of ways for climbing towards the upper strata of vegetation to get to the sun's rays.

Among the vines, for example, **climbing hempvine** sprawls over low trees along the water's edge, sometimes making them lean into the water. Its scalloped, three-inch leaves accompany a year-around bloom of very small white or pink flowers. **Climbing aster,** in contrast, is a deciduous vine that blooms in November and December, with a profusion of inch-long lavender flowers. Unlike most vines, it manages to climb without using tendrils, the thread-like sinews that wrap around the host plant to give the vine a "toehold" as it climbs.

In contrast to the vines, air plants (epiphytes) have severed all connections with the ground to form aerial gardens along the trunks and branches of trees. These plants are not parasitic; they use their larger neighbors merely for support at a sunnier level as they take nourishment from air and rain water.

Among air plants, the **butterfly orchid** is probably Florida's most common wild orchid. You'll see this air plant hanging from mangroves, pond apples, oaks and pines. Its five-starred leaves support a 1.5-inch flower, usually white on the lips and pink on the inside, making it look like a small butterfly wing. In contrast, you'll have to look along shorelines and in floating mats of vegetation for this foot-or-so-high **water spider orchid.** Its thick, succulent leaves are joined by small green flowers about 3-4th inch across. Their narrow petals make them look like small green spiders.

Spanish moss may be the most common of all "soil-less" plants in the park, but it is neither moss nor air plant. It uses long, thin, scaly stems to wrap around the host tree and hang down from the branches. The grayish leaves are covered with cup-like, permeable scales that "catch" moisture and nutrients from the air and store them up in "pockets" on the surface of the host tree. That's why they can stay alive in periods of drought.

Once upon a time, Spanish moss was harvested commercially to stuff mattresses and car seats. Today, songbirds use it for nest-building. Sometimes they even make nests *in* the moss clumps. But so, too, do redbugs and chiggers.

When you stand at the dock next to the River Campground you're in the midst of a tidal swamp - actually the Loxahatchee River in this case. Both sides are dominated by mangroves, which occupy 308 acres of riverfront before they give way to the ferns and cypress of the floodplain, the freshwater portion of the river described in the previous section.

What makes the two communities different is salt. Whereas the saline content in the ocean is around 35 parts per thousand (ppt), it takes far less salt to sustain a mangrove environment in the river. For example, at the park concession dock just above mile marker 6, the salt content can vary from 1 ppt in the rainy summer to 15 ppt in the dry winter. When salt's influence finally gives out around mile marker 9 upstream, the ferns and cypress of the floodplain take over.

Here's a closer look at the two types of mangrove seen in the park. **Red mangrove** is found nearest to the water because it has the highest salt resistance. You can spot it mainly by its arching "prop" roots, which help provide stability while also supplying air to the submerged roots. Red mangroves grow up to 20 feet. They have dark green elliptical leaves of three to five inches long and produce a dart-like fruit of up to a foot long. If one drops in the soft sand like an arrow – and sticks - it's ready to start growing and reproducing.

The **white mangrove,** which can attain 60-foot heights, has leaves that are smooth underneath and rounded at both base and tip. Just below the base are

Osprey

Red Mangrove

two little bumps, called nectarines that secrete a sugar that insects love. The white mangrove's fruit is a reddish brown, soft, fleshy pod with a dark red seed inside.

What all mangroves have in common is that their roots anchor the sand and peat along the water's edge. The roots also trap shells, leaves, bark and other river bottom debris so that young fish and shellfish can get something to eat without having to try their luck in dangerous deeper water. The continuous shedding of mangrove leaves and other plant components produce as much as 80 percent of the total organic material available in the aquatic food web.

Other vascular plants associated with the tidal swamp include **Gulf cordgrass, water hyssop** and **sea oxeye.**

Animals along the shoreline are the same prowlers described in the section on the floodplain swamp. But in the river itself are more salt-friendly species: **sponges, oysters, marine worms, barnacles, mangrove tree crabs,** and **fiddler crabs.** And if there's a log or branch protruding into the water, odds are that you'll find one of Florida's many **turtle** species catching some rays on it.

Mangrove Tree Crab

Fiddler Crab

Sea Oxeye

White Mangrove

Saltwater fish, which go up and down-river with the tides, include **snook, jack crevalle, tarpon, rays, ladyfish, menhaden, lookdown, permit, mangrove snapper, sheepshead, porgies,** and **mullet.** The latter include several species, among them the rare **mountain mullet.**

Mullet tend to be the most visible because they jump so much – especially in late fall when they head upstream in schools to spawn, usually chased all the way by hungry jack crevalles and snook.

Finally, you may see a prominent mammal cruising lazily just below the river's surface. If you see a snout break water every three or four minutes, look also for circular ripples like canoe paddles leave. Most likely you've gotten at least a glimpse of the **West Indian manatee,** a large, gray aquatic mammal with a body that tapers to a flat, paddle-shaped tail. Also called a sea cow, it has two forelimbs, or flippers, each with three to four nails.

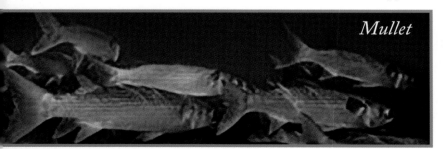

Mullet

The face is wrinkled with whiskers on the snout. Manatees are believed to have evolved from a wading, plant-eating animal and are most closely related to elephants.

The average adult is

Gina, the author's Jack Russell Terrier, says hello to a manatee at a river dock

Manatee

about 9 feet long and weighs between 800 to 1,200 pounds. It depends entirely on aquatic vegetation and can consume from 10 to 15 percent of its body weight daily.

When manatees are using a great deal of energy, they may surface to breathe as often as every 30 seconds. When resting, manatees have been known to stay submerged for up to 20 minutes.

Manatees can live 60 years or more. They often don't because so many suffer fatal collisions with speeding boats or from being crushed in canal locks or drowned in flood control structures. Today, there are only 3,000 or manatees left in the U.S. and Jonathan Dickinson, with its "NO WAKE" boating rules, remains one of their few sanctuaries.

Avoid these plants like poison!

The park has two plants whose sap is toxic to human skin. One is **poison ivy** with its familiar three leaves. The other is **poisonwood,** which is found only in scrub. Poisonwood

Poison Ivy

Poisonwood

belongs to the same plant family as poison ivy, but has five leaflets instead of three and produces orange berries the size of marbles. It produces a milky sap that causes blistering of the skin.

CHAPTER THREE
Activities in and around the Park

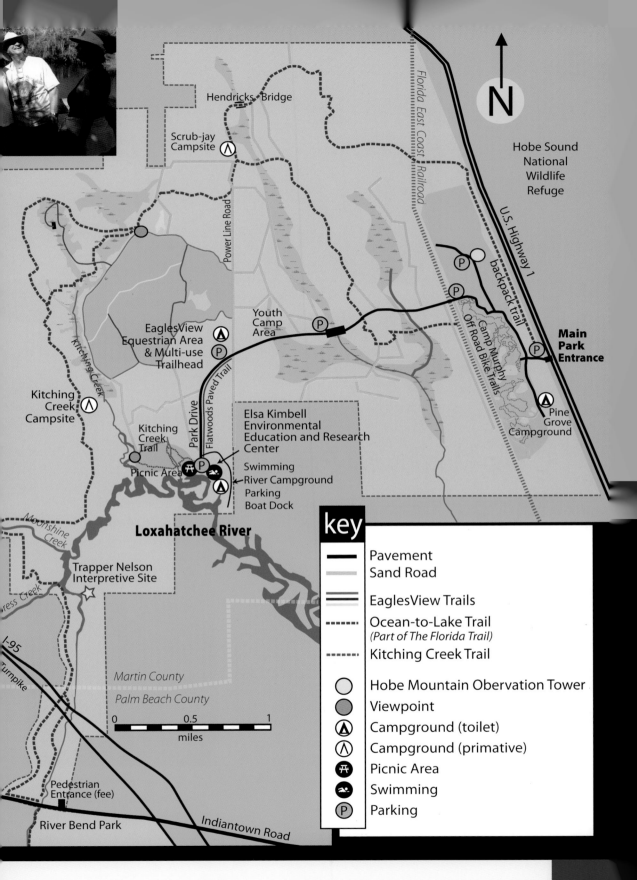

N

Hendricks Bridge

Scrub-jay Campsite

Florida East Coast Railroad

Hobe Sound National Wildlife Refuge

U.S. Highway 1

Power Line Road

Youth Camp Area

P

P

P

backpack trail

Camp Murphy Off Road Bike Trails

Main Park Entrance

P

EaglesView Equestrian Area & Multi-use Trailhead

P

Kitching Creek

Pine Grove Campground

Kitching Creek Campsite

Kitching Creek Trail

Park Drive

Flatwoods Paved Trail

Elsa Kimbell Environmental Education and Research Center

Picnic Area

P

Swimming
River Campground
Parking
Boat Dock

Moonshine Creek

Loxahatchee River

Trapper Nelson Interpretive Site

Cypress Creek

I-95

Turnpike

Martin County
Palm Beach County

| 0 | 0.5 | 1 |

miles

Pedestrian Entrance (fee)

River Bend Park

Indiantown Road

key

▬▬▬	Pavement
▬▬▬	Sand Road
≡≡≡	EaglesView Trails
- - - -	Ocean-to-Lake Trail *(Part of The Florida Trail)*
- - - -	Kitching Creek Trail
○	Hobe Mountain Obervation Tower
●	Viewpoint
Ⓐ	Campground (toilet)
Ⓐ	Campground (primitive)
⛺	Picnic Area
🏊	Swimming
Ⓟ	Parking

Camp Murphy Off Road Bicycle Trails

The park's varied and challenging network of bike trails have been created and maintained by Club Scrub, a group of enthusiastic cyclers affiliated with the nonprofit Friends of Jonathan Dickinson State Park.

One way to access the off-road bike trail system is to drive along the main paved road heading north until you come to the well-marked parking area just east of the railroad tracks. There you'll start pedaling the 1.6-mile Tortoise Trail heading southeast and connecting to other loops (see map).

The second way is to take the first immediate left after the park entrance (towards the Pine Grove Campground) and go right where the road forks. In seconds you'll be at the beginning of the 1.9 mile Middle Ridge bike trail. It's connected to the .9 mile Osprey loop.

At either entry point, thanks to the volunteers of Club Scrub, you'll find trail signs such as green for novice bikers, blue for intermediate and black for experts only.

A lone periwinkle sprouts through the cracked blacktop remains of a Camp Murphy road.

Camp Murphy
Off Road Bicycle Trails

—RIDE AT YOUR OWN RISK—
PLEASE!

- Wear An Approved Helmet.
- Stay On Marked Trail.
- Carry Plenty Of Drinking Water.
- Pass Other Riders With Care.
- Use Caution At Intersections.
- Observe Trail Direction Signs At All Times.

Trail Signs

- Green Novice
- Blue Intermediate
- Black Difficult Stunt Experts Only
- P Exit To Pavement Return To Parking

Front Section:

Trail	Miles
Tortoise	.8
Hare	.7
Ranger	.9
Lake	.3
Gator Hole	.1
Palmetto	.6
Bypass	.1
Fire Ring	.6
Prickly Pear	.1
Eight Tenths	.9
Silo	.3
Bunker Hill	.1
Total Miles	**5.4**

Back Section:

Trail	Miles
Middle Ridge	.6
Osprey Loop	1.7
Big Burn	.9
Total Miles	**3.2**
Front & Back	**8.6**

www.clubscrub.org

Hobe Mountain Observation Tower Trail

It's less than a half-mile long, but the Hobe Mountain Observation Tower Trail is your best bet for understanding the scrub/sandhill environment and getting the best overall view of the park short of renting a helicopter.

The walk will take you, by boardwalk, to the observation tower built upon an 86-foot dune that was once part of a ridge that made up the ancient Atlantic Ocean shoreline. Climb the tower, look west, and you'll see the same undisturbed landscape that Spaniards looked upon 500 years ago and Native Americans for some 5,000 years before the first Europeans arrived.

EaglesView Multi-Use Trail System

This eight-mile collection of trails was created mainly for equestrian use, but can be used by walkers and off-road bikers with the understanding that horses and their mounts get the right-of-way. For the same reason, the five camp sites, each with water and electricity, are reserved for those who bring in their own horses and trailers. (There are no for-hire stables in or near the park.)

EaglesView offers three well-marked trails: the yellow, blue and red. The latter two in part lead along the upper Kitching Creek. Restrooms at the trailhead are open to all.

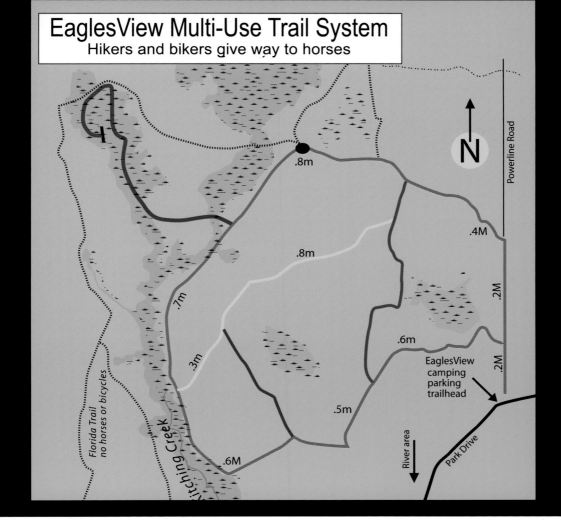

EaglesView Multi-Use Trail System
Hikers and bikers give way to horses

.8m

N

Powerline Road

.4M

.8m

.2M

.7m

.6m

.2M

.3m

EaglesView
camping
parking
trailhead

Florida Trail
no horses or bicycles

.5m

.2M

River area

Witching Creek

Park Drive

.6M

Flatwoods Paved Trail

Opened in 2007, this asphalt trail runs roughly parallel to the main road leading from the EaglesView trailhead to the Elsa Kimbell Environmental Education and Research Center. Currently about one mile long (not a loop), the trail will eventually be extended throughout the entire five miles between the Camp Murphy trailhead and riverfront facilities

This trail welcomes bikers, walkers and rollerbladers. It's also the best trail in the park for anyone using a wheelchair. Do note that at times of excessive rains, parts of the asphalt trail may be ankle-deep in water.

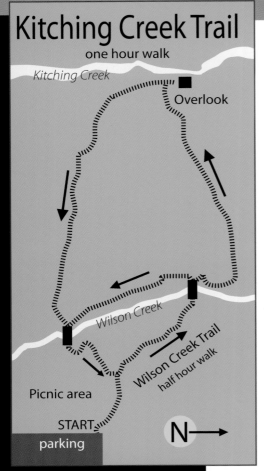

Kitching Creek Trail
one hour walk

Kitching Creek

Overlook

Wilson Creek

Wilson Creek Trail
half hour walk

Picnic area

START

parking

N→

Kitching Creek/ Wilson Creek Trail

Perhaps the most popular of walks in JDSP, it actually consists of two options. Starting in the picnic area, you can spend about a half-hour walking the small loop that revolves around the shallow, fern-filled Wilson Creek. Or you can start on the Wilson Creek trail and continue on to the platform overlooking cypress-lined Kitching Creek. The latter loop takes about an hour.

Kitching Creek was named for Walter Kitching, an English entrepreneur who bought the adjoining land from the state of Florida in 1886 for $1.25 an acre. At a time when there were no paved roads in south Florida, Kitching had established a thriving business by stocking a sailboat with groceries and selling them at dockside to settlers along the Indian River.

Actually, Kitching bought the land as a possible homestead for his sister in England. She never saw it. When World War II broke out, the U. S. military confiscated all the land around Kitching Creek for Camp Murphy.

Hikers enjoy the Kitching Creek Overlook

The Backpack Trail
(Portion of the Ocean-to-Lake Trail)

Within the park, this nearly 15-mile footpath is nicknamed the "Backpack Trail," but it's actually part of the 70-mile Ocean-to-Lake Trail that begins in Hobe Sound and meanders westward to the shore of Lake Okeechobee. There it ties into the 1,300 mile Florida National Scenic Trail running the length of the state.

All this is being developed by the 5,000-plus volunteer hiking enthusiasts who belong to the Florida Trail Association. FTA local chapters maintain some 24 miles of hiking trails within Jonathan Dickinson State Park, including our 14.5 mile portion of the Ocean-to-Lake segment.

It's roughly shaped like an arc, spreading westward from the park entrance parking lot, swinging to the north, then around to its western terminus in the upper Kitching Creek area. Now picture a north-south vertical line near the top of the arc and you have the Return Trail that brings you south to your starting point, allowing you to walk nine miles instead of the full 14.5.

The trails are well marked by orange blazes on trees, but even if you know your directions, you've got to be fit and hardy to attempt the Backpack Trail. The only facilities are two primitive campsites with no electricity. Each has a composting toilet and pitcher pump (water must be treated). One is the Scrub Jay campsite, located about mid-way near the Return Trail. The second is the Kitching Creek campsite, the terminus of the 14.5-mile hike.

For more information on the Florida Trail contact:

Florida Trail Association
P.O. Box 13708, Gainesville, FL 32604
Phone: 800-343-1882
www.floridatrail.org

The Upriver Canoe Trail

Canoes, kayaks and small motor boats are available for rent at the River Store. Or, you can haul your own craft to the put-in site near the River Campground.

Trapper Nelson's historic camp is just three or so miles upriver, but you'll have to contend with going against the current. And when rains have been recent and heavy, the stiffer the current becomes once you get up into the narrower reaches of the river. So be forewarned that getting there – and back – by canoe or kayak requires paddling skill, good conditioning and perhaps more time than you reckoned.

If that seems forbidding, consider a paddle up Kitching Creek. Thanks to the efforts of local landowners to resist logging in the 1940s, many cypress trees remain there, creating much the same pristine environment that you'd experience in the area around Trapper Nelson's.

Either way, take water and a snack, because there's nothing enroute.

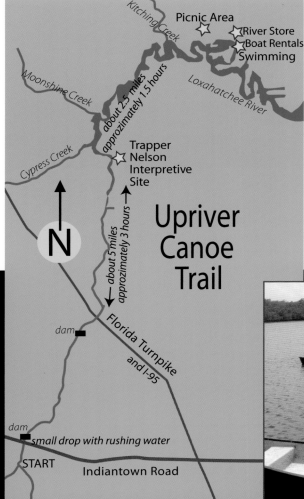

Kitching Creek
Picnic Area
River Store
Boat Rentals
Swimming
Moonshine Creek
about 2.5 miles
approzimately 1.5 hours
Loxahatchee River
Cypress Creek
Trapper Nelson Interpretive Site
about 5 miles
approzimately 3 hours
N
Upriver Canoe Trail
dam
Florida Turnpike and I-95
dam
small drop with rushing water
START
Indiantown Road

Cypress Canopy River Trail to Trapper Nelson's

This trail probably elicits more oohs and ahs than any in the park. But to get to the canoe/kayak put-in point, you'll need to drive out of the park, into the heart of Jupiter on U.S. 1 and up Indiantown Road until you are a half-mile west of the Florida Turnpike – a 15-mile ride in all. After a left turn at the "Canoe Rental" sign, you're on the edge of Palm Beach County's Riverbend Park.

There you rent or put in your own craft (no motors allowed) and glide down the brown-but-clear river heading north. Now you're in the southwestern reaches of JDSP in the storybook Tarzan-and-Jane country above the Trapper Nelson Interpretative Site. Here you'll be navigating narrow, sharp turns while careening your neck at the breathtaking canopy of bald cypress surrounding you on all sides. If the water is low, you may have to get out and push here and there. Yes, you may see alligators, but there's little danger as long as you don't try to offer one a fried chicken drumstick.

If you begin your trip from eight to ten in the morning, you can expect to arrive at the Trapper Nelson camp in time to enjoy your picnic during the "normal" lunchtime hours. The site offers Trapper's own jerrybuilt restrooms, a drinking fountain and a large covered pavilion with picnic tables - but that's about it. Don't expect a hamburger stand.

After taking time for the ranger's guided tour you can expect to spend another two hours paddling downstream until you finally reach the take-out ramp by the dock at the River Campground. If you've rented canoes or kayaks, Canoe Outfitters of Florida will have a bus wait-

Boat ramp and canoe take-out.

ing to take you back to Riverbend Park where you parked your car. If you brought your own watercraft, you'd better have a second car stashed in the boat ramp parking lot to get you back to the outfitters.

Biking

The roads of JDSP are all open to bikers, as are the many off-road trails described earlier. Club Scrub, a nonprofit group of biking enthusiasts, works hard to maintain the trails. Its rules-of-the-trail brochure is available at the ranger station.

Club Scrub sponsors several of its own races (usually followed by a "social,") and has also played host to bike fests attracting as many as 600 off-road aficionados. Check the park schedule to see if there's an event being held during your visit.

You can contact Club Scrub on line at:
www.clubscrub.org
or through

Friends of Jonathan Dickinson State Park, Inc.
16450 S. E. Federal Highway
Hobe Sound, FL 33455

www.friendsofjdsp.org.

Camping

Two family campgrounds are available. The Pine Grove Campground, located near the entrance on U.S. 1, offers 90 sites. The River Campground, a four-mile drive from the park entrance, offers 45 sites just back from the Loxahatchee River shoreline. Twelve cabins, just a stone's throw from the River Campground, are also available for rent at the River Store.

In addition, the park offers a primitive camping area for Scouts and other youth groups, subject to advance reservation. Finally, don't forget the primitive campsites mentioned in the Backpack Trail section of this chapter.

Swimming

Just down from the River Store you'll find a large beach with a cordoned-off area for swimming. The slope is gradual and it's safe from boats. From May through October you can expect water temperatures above 80 degrees. Only in the dead of an extra-cold winter does it get too frigid for comfort.

Children's play area

Just behind the River Store is a large compound with swings, seesaws and rides for young kids to enjoy themselves.

Fishing

The fishing is generally good in JDSP. Although you're most apt to bring in catfish, sheepshead and mangrove snappers, do note that the Loxahatchee is one of the world's best rivers for snook. And when you hook one (with the black strip the length of its middle) expect a two-footer or more.

Legally you can fish from shore anywhere in the park except at the canoe dock or the swimming area. You don't need a license, either, if you're fishing from land and have lived in Florida more than six months. Otherwise, it's off you go to the Martin County tax office or a local bait shop. The River Store sells neither fishing licenses nor gear.

The large dock near the River Campground is fine for fishing.

Jonathan Dickinson State Park differs from other state parks in that there is more to its trails than the "official" networks designated as safe, signed and regularly maintained. The reason for this is the legacy of Camp Murphy, which in its heyday was a latticework of roads carved out of the scrub and sandhills that parallel the railroad tracks in the park's eastern sector.

For example, heading south of the Camp Murphy Off Road Bicycle Trails you can continue on the rough road that parallels the tracks on the east side. Along the way you'll find many sugar sand pathways that lead up and down steep hills. It was in this sector that Camp Murphy had its rifle range and – just south of it – the steep hill into which recruits fired 50-caliber machine guns. Look west when climbing and you'll get a close-up look of the eerie Air Force dishes that track space launches on the park's southern rim. Look east and you may see a freight train lumbering slowly on the tracks below.

But do be forewarned. There are no trail signs, no water, no restrooms. Bikes bog down quickly in the thick sugar sand. Heavy rains can create instant swamps. Although you aren't very far from U.S. 1 or the lush greens of the neighboring Jupiter Hills Country Club, being amidst all that sand and pine can be disorienting. You *can* get lost!

Across the train tracks from the parallel bike trail loom two towers once used for wastewater treatment at Camp Murphy

Tour boat trips to Trapper Nelson Interpretive Site

The Loxahatchee Queen II is a 25-seat pontoon boat with regular tours to the Trapper Nelson Interpretive Site. You'll get a narrated tour about the river from the boat captain and, after you've disembarked at Trapper's dock, a guided walk through the site by a park ranger. A second, similar boat is available for private party charters.

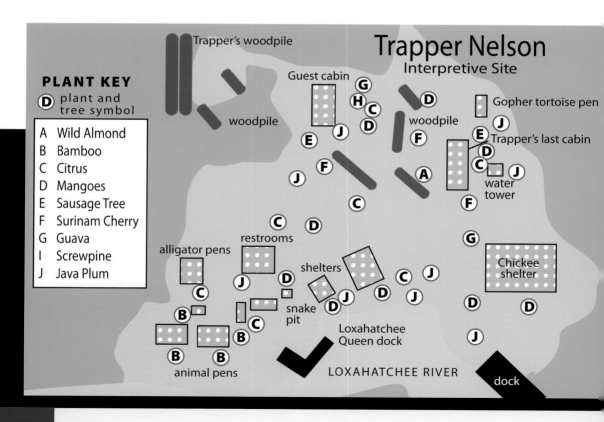

Trapper's woodpile

Trapper Nelson
Interpretive Site

Guest cabin

PLANT KEY

Ⓓ plant and tree symbol

A	Wild Almond
B	Bamboo
C	Citrus
D	Mangoes
E	Sausage Tree
F	Surinam Cherry
G	Guava
I	Screwpine
J	Java Plum

woodpile

woodpile

Gopher tortoise pen

Trapper's last cabin

water tower

restrooms

alligator pens

shelters

Chickee shelter

snake pit

animal pens

Loxahatchee Queen dock

LOXAHATCHEE RIVER

dock

Boating

The River Store will rent you three kinds of boat by the hour: canoes, kayaks and small motorboats (usually with 8 h.p. motors). You're free to take them as far upriver as Trapper Nelson's and down-river only to the park border (about a half-mile below the rental dock).

Elsa Kimbell Environmental Education and Research Center

The Center, opened in 2006, is a tribute to the late Elsa Kimbell, a tireless volunteer for the state park system. As president of Friends of Jonathan Dickinson State Park, she spearheaded the effort to create a center of environmental learning within JDSP.

The Center today can help you learn about South Florida nature in many ways. Outside, staff members conduct regular nature walks. They also sponsor school and family tours such as going to a nearby pond and discovering what lives in it. Once samples are collected, the group goes back to the Center's lab and analyzes their specimens under microscopes.

Inside the Center are ever-changing exhibits enabling viewers to learn more about the plant and animal life they discover in their park walks. Also inside is a large meeting hall capable of seating large audiences for special lectures. Visit the lobby and pick up some literature on what's going on during your visit.

There's also lots to do in the neighborhood!

If you'd like to venture beyond JDSP's boundaries, you'll find several sites that can help you experience local environment and history (in addition to the usual shopping centers and cinemas). Within a 20 mile, half-hour radius from the park are the following places, beginning here with the farthest north, traveling south on U.S. 1, and then up Indiantown Road to the westernmost site.

TANAH KEETA SCOUT RESERVATION

Tanah Keeta Scout Reservation is very close to the River Campground area. Its one square mile was carved from the park in 1953 by Congress in order to create a camping complex for the Gulf Stream Council of Boy Scouts. It's equipped with cabins, campfire rings and a large community hall. You may hear the shouts of Scouts as they splash in their swimming pool or paddle on the Loxahatchee from their large dock.

Contact:
8501 Boy Scout Road, Tequesta, FL 33469. Phone: 561-746-8749.

CAMP WELAKA

Camp Welaka lies far up the North Fork of the Loxahatchee River, just beyond County Line Road, where it borders on JDSP. Like the older Boy Scout camp (above) its square mile (640 acres) was created from state park land over 50 years ago. Today it is a wooded campus of cabins, platform tents, mess hall, swimming-canoeing lake and riverfront boardwalk.

Contact:
Girl Scouts of Palm Glades Council, 1224 W. Indiantown Road, Jupiter, FL 33458.

LORAN TOWER

North of the Hobe Mountain Obervation Tower you'll see a tall slim tower that blinks red around the clock. No, it's not a cell phone tower. It's one of 84 stations operated by the U.S. Department of Transportation to detect positions of ships and aircraft by analyzing pulsed radio signals from two or more ground stations. The system was earmarked for extinction in 2000 due to the advent of Global Positioning Satellites, but technical problems with GPS have prolonged the life of LORAN towers.

Ever vigilant satellite dishes

Besides its famous seasprays, Blowing Rocks Preserve offers quiet trails along the Intracoastal Waterway

MISSILE TRACKING SITE

In 1985 the park ceded 11 acres in its southeastern corner for one of several coastal stations that track satellite and missile launches as they roar off from Cape Canaveral. Replacing an older site in Grand Bahama, the Jonathan Dickinson Missile Tracking Annex is operated by the Air Force Research and Development Command. Look up in the southern part of the park and you'll see the four telemetry dishes brooding overhead like giant mushrooms.

ST. LUCIE INLET STATE PARK

First, don't even think about going there unless you can bring a kayak, canoe or motorboat. If you do, take U.S. 1 north to Cove Road in Stuart and then east (right) until you reach the Intracoastal (Indian River). From there it's a quarter-mile punt across to the many docks at the state park. A long boardwalk then leads you to one of the most pristine ocean beaches in South Florida.

On a typical weekday you can walk the beach to unspoiled St. Lucie Inlet without seeing a soul. If you bring your kayak/canoe, you can paddle north from the public docks, turn right (east) into the inlet, and make another right into Hole in the Wall, a secluded, shallow lagoon where you'll see a profusion of ibis, roseate spoonbills and other wading birds.

For more info:
772-219-1880 or
floridastateparks.org/stlucieinlet.

BLOWING ROCKS PRESERVE

Go south on U.S. 1 to Beach Road in Tequesta and take the bridge east that puts you on the southern tip of 16-mile-long Jupiter Island. Head north and you'll soon see the headquarters of this 73-acre Nature Conservancy preserve on your left.

Besides protecting a variety of natural habitats, the sanctuary's most interesting feature is occupying the largest rocky Anastasia limestone shoreline on the Atlantic coast. Due to cavities created in the limestone by constant wave action, high tides and breaking seas can produce plumes of saltwater up to 50 feet in the air. Hence the name "Blowing Rocks."

More info:
772-744-6668.

HOBE SOUND NATIONAL WILDLIFE REFUGE

If you'd like to experience the western shoreline along the Indian River, JDSP's nearest neighbor awaits you. Head north up U.S. 1 and the wildlife sanctuary's parking lot and headquarters is just two miles south of Bridge Road in Hobe Sound. Here you can walk through 300 acres of endangered sand pine scrub, some of it leading along the Indian River shore. The headquarters building contains an exhibit room, gift shop and environmental education room.

For more info:
772-546-6141
or www.fws.gov/
hobesound.

Jupiter Inlet Lighthouse

JUPITER INLET LIGHTHOUSE & MUSEUM

This is where it all began. Today some six million people and who knows how many winter visitors live in the 250-mile coastal strip between Titusville and Key Biscayne. But in 1853, when Congress authorized a lighthouse at Jupiter Inlet, that same area contained less than 600 souls. Today southeast Florida's oldest active building still sends its beacon out each night. The 125-acre lighthouse grounds contains the Loxahatchee River Historical Society headquarters, a museum of local history and a riverfront History Corridor containing an old settler home and other artifacts. You can tour the lighthouse and surrounding attractions for one reasonable ticket price.

More info:
561-747-8380 or www.lrhs.org.

DUBOIS PARK AND JUPITER BEACH PARK

Why these two lovely parks have separate names is a mystery because they're joined together and are both maintained by Palm Beach County. The only difference is that 18.7-acre DuBois Park fronts along the southern shore of Jupiter Inlet, whereas 46.5- acre Jupiter Beach Park lies along the oceanfront.

The two parks are separated by a shallow tidal lagoon to which local parents love to take their toddlers for wading. This lagoon is actually the remains of the original Jupiter Inlet, into which the Spanish explorer Ponce de Leon sailed in 1513.

Both parks have picnic areas. What distinguished the two: DuBois Park is a good venue for watching boats going in and out of the inlet. It's also the site of the Dubois House, an 1889 homestead built on ancient Indian mounds by one of Jupiter's first families. Jupiter Beach Park includes the jetty, with facilities for ocean fishing. Beyond the beach are reefs that snared several Spanish gold ships in the days of yore. Who knows what riches may still lay out there?

Directions: U.S. 1 south to the first street after you cross the Loxahatchee River (Carlin White) Bridge. For Dubois Park, go about a mile and left at Dubois Road sign. For Jupiter Beach Park, continue east another half mile and go left on the last road or you'll smack into a sand dune.

For more info on Dubois Park: 561-747-8380 or www.pbcgov.com/parks/locations/dubois. Jupiter Beach Park: 561-966-6600 or www.pbcgov.com/parks/locations/jupiterbeach

LOXAHATCHEE RIVER ENVIRONMENTAL CENTER

Heading south from the Jupiter Lighthouse on U.S. 1, cross the Carlin White Bridge and make a left at the second stop light. There, in Burt Reynolds Park, is a large gray building that hosts children's tours and field study for the Jupiter High School Environmental Research & Field Studies Academy. It's sponsored by the Loxahatchee River District, which treats the area's wastewater and monitors the river's water quality.

Open to all visitors, the River Center has exhibits and a touch tank focusing on marine and estuarine ecosystems.

More info:
561-744-7995
or www.loxahatcheeriver.org.

LOGGERHEAD MARINELIFE CENTER

Take U.S. 1 to the first stoplight on the south side of the Carlin White river bridge and head east on A1A. In about four miles you'll come to Juno Beach and this nonprofit sea turtle rehabilitation and education facility on the west side of the road.

Exhibits include a giant Leatherback sea turtle, salt water aquaria and displays of local wildlife. The building also includes a marine-oriented gift shop full of local crafts and educational books. The surrounding campus offers a guarded beach, nature trails and picnic pavilions.

More info:
561-627-8280
or www.marinelife.org.

JOHN D. MACARTHUR BEACH STATE PARK

Take U.S. 1 south to PGA Boulevard, go east to highway A1A and in 2.8 miles you're at the entrance of this 325-acre park. A gateway to two miles of pristine beach, it is also a unique mixture of coastal and tropical hammock and mangrove forest. Facilities include a nature center and gift shop.

The western part of the park fronts on 22-mile-long Lake Worth and its historically interesting Munyon Island. Rangers conduct kayak trips to the island and other parts of the inland lagoon.

More info:
561-624-6952 or www.florida-stateparks.org/macarthurbeach.

Busch Wildlife Sanctuary director David Hitzig exhibits one of the sanctuary's residents.

Kayaker in Riverbend Park

BUSCH WILDLIFE SANCTUARY AT OTTER CREEK

This environmental education center focuses on the Loxahatchee River's freshwater and upland ecosystem. Sponsored by the Loxahatchee River District, it includes an interpretative education center, a wildlife refuge, nature trails, gift shop and picnic tables.

Along the nature trails are aviaries and cages of live animals native to the area. Because the Sanctuary is a leading animal rescue and rehab facility, many of the animals on exhibit are those that couldn't be returned to the wild. Because this is as close as Jupiter comes to having a zoo, it's a very popular venue for families with small children.

More info: 561-575-3399 or www.loxahatcheeriver.org.

RIVERBEND PARK

Head west on Jupiter's Indiantown Road, a mile beyond the Florida Turnpike, and on your left is the entrance to one of Florida's most exquisite outdoor "works of art." Palm Beach County acquired this 680-acre former orange grove and trailer park in 1995 and kept it closed to the public for a dozen years while exotic growth was removed and the hydrology (water flow) returned to its natural state. Thousands of trees were planted as well.

The result today is almost as if Walt Disney had designed it. A five-mile waterway loop links creeks and ponds. Bike and walking trails cover some 15 miles, with convenient bypaths for tailoring a trip to your desires. As you walk, ride or paddle amidst all this, the number of turkey, deer, sandhill cranes, wood storks, and other wildlife may cause you to think you're on the set of *Bambi*.

More info:
561-746-7053
or www.co.palm-beach.fl/parks/locations/riverbend.

Also note: canoes and kayaks can be rented from Canoe Outfitters of Florida near the park entrance.

Phone: 561-746-7053
or www.canoeskayaksfla.com.

Chapter Four
The Struggle to Remain

A behind the scenes look at park management

Most visitors see state park management in terms of uniformed rangers doing routine tasks such as collecting fees, fielding questions and replacing signs. In fact, rangers are just the most visible part of a team of biologists, volunteers and district office experts who are all waging a constant struggle to maintain the park's wild and scenic ecology against an on-slaught of human and natural forces.

What any member of that team does in a given day is driven by a comprehensive Unit Management Plan developed for each Florida state park. Take a closer look at some of these priorities and chances are you'll have a new perspective on what you see all around you in the park and the people who work there.

Wild & Scenic

Blackened growth gives way to green shoots and new wildlife

Prescribed burns: fighting fire with fire

In several areas of Jonathan Dickinson State Park you've probably noticed blackened tree trunks and ground cover. Your first thought may be that someone's been very careless or that the rangers aren't very good at fire safety.

Not so. The Florida Park Service is charged with perpetuating the natural communities on state lands, and "prescribed burns" are one of the management tools available to rangers and the outside teams of fire specialists who often help them.

Why? Forestry experts have realized for many years now that the old policy of preventing all forest fires allowed dead, dry underbrush to accumulate. When ignited by lightning or some other unplanned combustion, this vegetative tinderbox became a powerful fuel that helped the fire spread. And when fallen limbs piled up around a tree — or dead needles hung from its branches — they could allow fires to climb this "fuel ladder" and destroy even the tallest canopy. JDSP learned its lesson in 1971 when a lightning fire raged out of control, jumped across U.S. 1, burned parts of Hobe Sound and could be seen by people on Hutchinson Island twenty miles away. When the smoke cleared, it had burned nearly 4,000 acres, or roughly one-third of the entire park.

Since then nearly 200 prescribed burns have taken place. A comprehensive fire management plan has organized the park into burn zones with objectives for each one. Examples: burning frequency, preferred season, smoke management criteria and special safety concerns.

The term *prescribed* means that before undertaking any burn, the project team must carefully calculate how fire will be applied to the various biological communities under selected weather conditions to accomplish predetermined management objectives. In each case the burn team must produce a written plan and obtain permission from the Florida Division of Forestry. Finally, backup firefighting services are put on standby alert.

As the science of prescribed burns has grown, so have the added benefits that can be documented. A major one is the restoration of natural communities. In the absence of fire, young broad-leafed hardwoods would begin growing in the shade of pine trees. As they matured, they would block out the light needed by pine seedlings and eventually take over the area as old pines died off. But young hardwoods have little resistance to fire, and the prescribed burns keep them at bay.

Another benefit is clearing the way for fire-adapted animals that depend on open ground. Examples: gopher tortoises, Florida scrub-jays and the Florida mouse. Birds such as quail, meadowlark and Bachman's sparrow are gone today because there wasn't enough burning to maintain an open habitat. The rare Florida mouse doesn't climb well, so the higher the shrubs the harder a time it has foraging for food. Burning regenerates a pine forest by removing competing vegetation so seedlings can become established, and by providing more open habitat for plants and animals.

Now put all this together in terms a gopher tortoise would understand. If hardwoods become too thick, Mr. Tortoise is forced to move out of the area. The post-fire landscape exposes seedlings to the sunlight. This stimulates growth of succulent shoots and softens the soil for burrow construction.

Sometimes, however, burning must be used in partnership with other management tools. A good example at JDSP is the large band of sand pine scrub that lines the eastern boundary on U.S. 1. Originally, it was a nearly treeless scrub ecosystem. Today's forest of sand pines grew before prescribed fire technology was developed. Now, with busy traffic on U.S. 1, the entrenched trees can't be burned off without the chance of smoke causing a highway hazard to drivers. The best alternative, called for in the park's Unit Management Plan, is to clear-cut the sand pines and scatter their tops and cones over the area. Only after chopping to reduce the dense understory of vegetation does prescribed burning begin.

These management techniques, followed by more-easily-managed burns, will eventually restore the biological integrity of the scrub ecosystem. In a fire's aftermath, the cones of sand pines will open and their seeds will be released to germinate on the bare mineral soil. Oaks will regenerate from root stock and acorns brought in by scrub-jays and other animals.

Brazilian pepper

Old World climbing fern

Invasive species: a never ending war

Invasive, or exotic, species are non-native plants and animals that came to Florida as a result of human-related activities. Exotics have fewer natural enemies and can rapidly displace native plants and animals. They may also harbor diseases or parasites that prey on non-resistant native species.

Because South Florida is one of the world's busiest destinations, plants and animals — like people — arrive literally from everywhere on earth. In the 1890s, the first "winter people" in Palm Beach sought out **water hyacinths** from their gardens up north because they thought they'd look pretty in their tropical ponds. Today water managers spend millions annually removing hyacinths from waterways, and the Loxahatchee is no exception. Lately the headlines have given way to news stories of pythons and boa constrictors showing up in state parks – most of them having been sold by retailers, only to be turned loose "out there somewhere" when their buyers found them to have grown too large and ornery.

But what rangers deal with in JDSP is more apt to fly or crawl under the publicity radar. **Brown anoles** from Cuba have declared war on their native green cousins. The **Cuban tree frog** actually eats the smaller native variety and is rapidly displacing them. But of all the exotic animal species, the biggest nuisance is one with a long history in Florida. When the Spanish took to their ships in 1783 as the English prepared to take over the territory, they left behind hundreds of domesticated hogs. Today their porcine progeny roam the wetter areas of JDSP. One feral hog, in his endless search for plant roots and whatever its thick snout can bulldoze leaves a trail of upturned plants (some of them endangered species) and deep hoof gouges that cause soil erosion. Small wonder that a regular part of a ranger's routine is setting and checking hog traps.

Damage left by feral hogs

Fighting exotic plant species is a more constant grind. Of the 173 exotic plants identified in JDSP, 37 are targeted for intensive — usually chemical — treatment. Why? Because they quickly form monocultures and outcompete and replace native plant communities. At the beginning of each fiscal year the park manager and biologists decide which sectors will receive focused treatment for the upcoming year. Once underway, a follow-up monitoring program takes place in each treated zone. It involves walking the area and removing newly established plants. As the park proceeds further along with its plan, more staff time will be shifted from treating areas towards providing follow-up efforts.

The major offenders today are **Old World climbing fern**, **downy rose myrtle** (even fire can't stop it), **melaleuca** (it sucks water like a drunken sailor), **Brazilian pepper** (grows like a weed), **Australian pines** (gracefully tall, but apt to topple in storms), and **strawberry guava** (a prolific seed producer).

To give you an idea of how much time biologists and rangers spend battling these plants, consider the Old World climbing fern. If you see a green vine-like blanket covering whole acres of trees, it's probably this voracious newcomer. Old World climbing fern was introduced to this part of Florida in 1965 and is now spreading at an alarming rate. An aerial survey conducted by the South Florida Water Management District in 1993 showed the fern covering an estimated 25,000 acres within the agency's jurisdiction. Just four years later, another survey found the fern covering 107,000 acres – a 328% growth. Here in Jonathan Dickinson, Old World climbing fern was first spotted along Kitching Creek in the early 1970s. It has now invaded virtually every type of plant community.

What makes this exotic so "successful" (from its point of view) is an amazing reproductive system. A single leaflet can produce over 26,000 spores year-around, each capable of establishing a new population wherever the wind blows it. Moreover, a spore seems happy to germinate in dead logs, fern tussocks, moist soil or even an indentation conveniently cultivated by a rooting hog.

One-time "Ornamental Gardens" site where invasive species were replaced with native plants

And it's not called "climbing fern" for nothing. As the elongated vines begin smothering other plants, they create a potential "flame ladder" that can carry fires into the crowns of trees. And as small pieces of fern material break off and drift with the heat thermals, they ignite spot fires wherever they land.

So far, it's been an uphill battle, as has the fight for manpower and money to do the job. Currently, teams of rangers, biologists or private contractors go out periodically and spray with commercial herbicides, which is why you may see clumps of dead vines along your walks. If the treatment teams can attack a small, new growth area, two applications a few months apart can usually stop it. But large, well-established areas are something else. Another park reports spraying one heavily-infested area eleven times, with re-sprouts and new growth continuing to pop up after each treatment.

Saving, promoting native species

A considerable part of a park ranger or biologist's job is simply monitoring and taking inventory of what's out there. It's all part of maintaining the list of plants and animals in the park. Sometimes the species data is plugged into broader studies being conducted by universities and state or national agencies. Sometimes it's necessary to determine if a certain species should be deemed endangered and in need of special protective efforts.

For example, in 1983 a park biologist reported that red-cockaded woodpeckers suddenly seemed to have disappeared. A study was launched to learn the cause and the park's Unit Management Plan was soon amended to make restoration of these popular visitor attractions one of its goals. The woodpeckers (not to be confused with the more common red-bellied woodpecker) still haven't returned, but hope remains. Trees with cavities that had housed their nests were marked and mapped. Today the trees still receive special treatment prior to prescribed burns by raking around the trunks to remove flammable debris.

The Florida scrub-jay also helps illustrate how bringing back a coveted park resident can take lots of time and patience. In 1981, when biologists conducted a statewide scrub-jay population survey, they observed 98 birds and estimated the park's total population at 200. By 1994 another survey showed a mere dozen birds. Learning why required years of banding scrub-jays and observing their patterns. Today there's no doubt that the bird's health and numbers depend on having open sandy soil on which to forage and from which to keep a nervous eye on any hawks that might be circling overhead. As sand pines and scrub oaks were allowed to take over the open space and cover the ground with fallen limbs and vegetation, the scrub-jays voted with their wings. Now, it's hoped that aggressive burns and removal of many trees will entice them back, along with gopher tortoises and all the critters that make their homes in the burrows that they vacate.

Sometimes an inventory of park assets can lead to a special effort to protect what's already there. Because encroaching saltwater in the river has destroyed many bald cypress trees, volunteers have helped park rangers plant more than 4,500 bald cypress seedlings in hopes of reversing the trend.

Florida Scrub-jay

In the 1980s it came to the attention of those who manage the federally-endangered species list in Washington that the four-petal pawpaw apparently grew only in Martin and Palm Beach counties – and not much even there. In 1988, they formed a pawpaw survey team, which found 230 mature plants growing in JDSP. The four-petal pawpaw went on the Endangered Species list – a big event in the biology world – and with it came a special obligation among JDSP managers to preserve and expand it. The responsibility includes taking annual population surveys, mapping locations, planting new seeds to expand the plants' range within the park, and making sure that the water table doesn't sink and parch them. Sorry, but we can't publicize their locations. Too many visitors seem to enjoy cutting endangered species and taking them home as souvenirs.

Sometimes the most one can do is to observe the presence of a given species and throw a protective shield around it. The American bald eagle, for example, in a typical year, anywhere from one to three or four adult bald eagles are seen in the park between October and April. A breeding pair is acutely vulnerable to disturbance from the start of courtship through egg laying, incubation and early brooding. If the pair feels threatened by anything, it may simply abandon the nest and leave the eggs or young ones to the elements. That's why the park follows guidelines issued by the U.S. Fish and Wildlife Service. They forbid any human activity within a 750-foot radius from the nest during the period described above.

One other way of protecting native species in the park is through the process of *mitigation*. Basically, mitigation means that if park management must unavoidably destroy native habitat, it's required to plant or restore the equivalent somewhere else. Thus, when the Florida Park Service decided to re-open the old swimming beach just down from the concession area, it meant removing some 200 feet of red mangroves along the river. Upstream, about a half mile beyond the entrance to Kitching Creek, a lady from Palm Beach had owned a weekend retreat in the 1950s that bordered on Trapper Nelson's land. She called her place "Ornamental Gardens" because it was full of royal palms, screw pines, bamboo and other pretty vegetation that, alas, had nothing to do with native foliage.

By the 21st century the long-abandoned homestead had left its mark in the form of entrenched, spreading exotic species. So it was an easy choice for the Park Service to choose a mitigation site for its beach project. Out went the exotics in went native cabbage palms, mangroves and other native species.

Finally, sometimes park management's mandate is simply to leave things alone. In the northwest corner of JDSP stands 2,600 acres designated as a State Wilderness Preserve. It's been left undisturbed by humans, but with a prayer that the Old World climbing fern doesn't find out about it.

CHAPTER FOUR: *The Struggle to Remain Wild and Scenic*

Keeping a lid on 'People Pollution'

Just when a ranger thinks his/her day is nicely planned, things can happen. Canoeists report hundreds of dead fish floating upstream. Rangers investigate and trace the source to spraying along ditches in an orange grove just beyond the park's border. Months later, a farm's aerial spraying creates another fish kill. Or:

- A call comes in that a truck has just overturned where Interstate I-95 crosses the river. A hundred gallons of diesel fuel spills out, requiring placement of temporary berms along the river banks.
- Two men are caught harvesting their own marijuana patch in the park's most remote wilderness section.
- Immigrants are arrested and fined for walking the park with machetes, whacking berries from saw palmettos and selling them to vitamin makers for male prostate preparations.
- A young macho poacher decides to hunt deer with a bow and arrow.
- A sweet elderly lady ambles about the park picking endangered dancing lady orchids.

All the above are based on actual reports filed by park rangers and biologists. Then there are day-to-day encroachments by residential neighbors that so often don't get noticed: dumping yard waste across the backyard fence, letting dogs and cats roam on park property, allowing backyard exotics to spread seeds into the park, or creating excessive noise for park visitors and wildlife alike.

Often the job of preserving the park means taking on businesses and government alike. In the early 1970s it took months to persuade the Florida Department of Transportation not to run Interstate 95 through the middle of the Trapper Nelson tract. In 1978 a still-controversial decision was made to allow the neighboring Jupiter Hills Club to withdraw over a million gallons a day from nearby ponds on park property. Later, however, park management refused the Village of Tequesta's request to dig wells in the park for drinking water and said no to the homeowners of Hobe Hills to the north when their association wanted to drain stormwater into the park.

Thankfully, the commissioners of Palm Beach and Martin counties have backed the JDSP staff in rejecting several proposals that might have doomed the park. In 1972, for example, a citizens group (unsuccessfully) urged the County Commission to alleviate noise around Palm Beach International airport by carving 4,000 or so acres from the park and building a massive new regional airport.

Issues like these and fighting dozens of lesser proposals to re-zone wetlands for agricultural land are why Park Service personnel sometimes seem to spend as much of their time in public hearings as they do planning trails and picnic areas.

These intrepid kayakers rest on the roof of Trapper Nelson's boat shed after the "Great Deluge" of October 20, 1995. During those 24-hours some 30 inches of rain fell on the JDSP area, overwhelming the Loxahatchee River in what was called a "once-in-a-century" event.

Damage control: coping with natural calamities

When a natural disaster occurs, all work-in-progress quickly gives way to the task of simply making park roads and campsites open to visitors. When it rained 30 inches during a 24-hour period on October 20-21,1995, the Loxahatchee River became the only way for most of the area's stormwater to reach the sea. That this was an enormous task for one river can be seen from the adjacent photo. These kayakers are resting atop the boathouse at Trapper Nelson's, about eight feet above the usual water level. Needless to say, much of the park was inundated for weeks.

Hurricanes create a different type of damage: trees snapped in two, limbs breaking power lines, branches lying askew across miles of park roads and trails. For example, after Hurricane Irene in 1999, a damage assessment showed a 16 percent loss of all sand pines in the park. When Wilma delivered a knockout blow in 2005, no one even had time for a damage survey.

In a federally-protected state park with a wild and scenic river and a wilderness preserve, there's a certain stoicism that one must accept and adapt to what Mother Nature decides to mete out. It explains why you won't see rangers out chopping up fallen trees except for those that block roads and major trails.

Keeping the fresh water flowing

Before road building and development truncated its natural flow, the Loxahatchee River Basin probably consisted of 500 square miles. Today it's commonly assumed to be a 240-square-mile watershed. The keys to avoiding further reduction are retaining sufficient wetlands acreage, maintaining the groundwater level high enough and storing water so as to keep the Loxahatchee's supply of freshwater flowing steadily during dry periods.

When farmers or developers ditch and drain the wetlands, the river is affected by:

- surges of stormwater that would otherwise be stored in the wetlands;
- a reduction in the volume of water that reaches the river via seepage;
- lowering the quality of water flowing into the river;
- reducing habitat for fish and wildlife.

At the same time, a smaller water flow brings the twin threats of fire and increased vegetation. Blazes from drying muck can devastate the riverside forest community, leaving only charred cypress skeletons. Moreover, a river can choke to death in its own vegetation if there's not enough current to sweep the slowly encroaching upland plants from its banks. Eventually, it becomes little more than an extended marsh.

All this is why an ongoing goal of the park's Unit Management Plan, or master blueprint, is to monitor all adjoining drainage canals for their impact on the Loxahatchee. Because many of them altered historical drainage patterns, they've burdened the river with silt, turbidity and pesticides. In addition, farms, residential developments and golf courses have combined to lower the groundwater table as they drill into the aquifers below.

Thankfully, many other local organizations have come to recognize these facts. In 2000 a new coalition, the Loxahatchee River Preservation Initiative (LRPI), began spearheading several projects using matching state funds. One of them sent a team to an old citrus grove to install a shoreline buffer of native floodplain vegetation and restore the natural water flow.

Old bridge on Kitching Creek where water flow was choked off by development

1940: Vegetative communities along the northwest fork of the Loxahatchee River

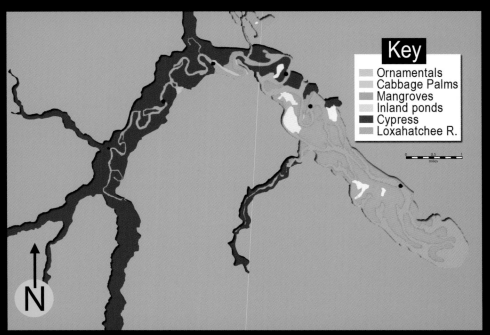

1995: How encroaching salt water altered river vegetation over 55 years

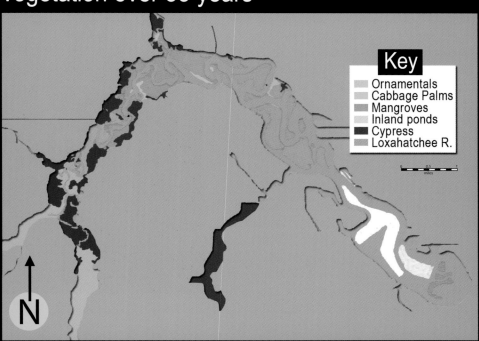

Another project aimed at unclogging upper Kitching Creek, whose flow had been greatly reduced when Bridge Road was extended westward in Hobe Sound. In the case of Cypress Creek, a major tributary, the LRPI began correcting ditching and development upstream that had caused a tremendous runoff that brought sediments and shoaling as the creek entered the Loxahatchee near the Trapper Nelson Interpretive Site.

So far, we've been discussing water flowing *towards* the sea. But salt water flowing *from* the sea is of equal concern to park managers. From the ancient Indian days through to the 1950s the shoreline opposite the River Campground (River Mile 6.5) consisted almost wholly of cypress, ferns and other fresh water plants. But soon thereafter people began to notice a new mangrove-salt water environment in the area. One reason was that Jupiter Inlet, closed during World War II (partly for fears of German sabotage), re-opened in 1947 and sent seawater further upriver. A few years later, when a larger U.S. 1 bridge was built, it deepened the riverbed and again increased the flow of seawater upstream. In the early 1970s residents living along canals near the abandoned Old Dixie Highway bridge wanted deeper water for their fishing boats, so they petitioned local authorities to remove the shallow oyster beds that surrounded the old bridge foundation. When the petition succeeded, even more saltwater flowed upriver. The combined effect was that the line of purely fresh water was pushed back to River Mile 9 just below Trapper Nelson's camp. It didn't take long for mangroves to take over the environment.

Bear in mind that despite irregular surges due to storms and hurricanes, the water flowing *downriver* was waning during this period. Moreover, it had usually been low during the dry winter season to begin with. It was obvious that the saltwater-mangrove environment was bound to creep even further upriver unless something were done. With the Florida Park Service and the South Florida Water Management District working together, some three years of study and public hearings led to a report setting a goal of maintaining a downstream flow of from 50 to 110 cubic feet per second during the dry season. If that could be achieved, said the computer models, the river system would eventually consist of four main sectors:

1. Cypress swamp and hydric hammock in the freshwater floodplain from River Mile 16 to 9.5 (upstream of Hobe Grove Ditch).
2. Cypress swamp in a tidal, mostly freshwater floodplain (River Mile 9.5 to 5.5 near the Boy Scout camp).
3. A mesohaline (brackish) zone, receptive to oysters, from River Mile 5.5 to 4.0.
4. A predominately saltwater (polyhaline) zone from River Mile 4.0 to the Inlet that supports sea grass and nourishes saltwater species.

So far it's still a work in progress. But armed with this new knowledge, you can look out over the river and understand the silent drama taking place.

The monitoring station at the mouth of Kitching Creek

Keeping it clean: monitoring and preservation of water quality

If you should arrive by water to the entrance of Kitching Creek you'll see a tall post supporting a metal container. Actually, it's one of three stations, installed by the U.S. National Geological Survey along the Wild & Scenic portion of the river, that monitor 30 parameters of water quality. They include such factors as salinity, turbidity and dissolved oxygen.

In addition, the local water quality watchdog, the Loxahatchee River District, maintains a network of more than 40 monitoring stations. Several are operated by volunteers who each dip a bucket of river water from the docks behind their homes, conduct various tests and send in weekly reports as to what they find.

All of this underscores that maintaining the flow of fresh water isn't of much use unless it's of decent quality. The scientific gauges and volunteers represent a front-line defense against what can threaten that quality: oil and grease from roads, pesticides and fertilizers from farms and surges of untreated water after heavy rains.

Volunteer water sampling

Do Not Disturb:
The delicate task of preserving cultural and archeological sites

You are visiting an area that has been populated longer than Rome and perhaps even longer than the Tigris-Euphrates river basin. In all there are 74 recorded archeological sites in the Loxahatchee watershed. Twenty four are within the park boundaries. At least thirty lie within adjacent Riverbend Park, which borders the upper river southwest of the Florida Turnpike and I-95.

Some sites were made by the ancient Jeaga and Miaymi Indians. Some appear to have been villages elevated by earth thrown up when canals were dug to speed canoe travel between settlements. They could contain the remains of separate buildings used for housing, for rituals and for burials. Some may represent only campsites used by hunting parties and families to and from their summer hiatus near the ocean.

Other sites represent Seminole Indian settlements in the 1800s and some mark important battles when the Second Seminole Indian War was decided around Jupiter. The key battle, for example, was fought on January 24, February 1838 in an area just west of I-95 where Indiantown Road crosses the Loxahatchee.

Okay, so how can you go explore these places? It's a delicate question. Even though many are registered on the Florida Master File of archeological sites, park managers are loathe to tell you exactly where they are for two reasons. First, the records are full of case histories of people churning up and trampling sites in search of artifacts they can sell to collectors. Second, the park lacks the budget dollars to protect the sites. Meanwhile, you'll have to be content with visiting the Trapper Nelson site and the remnants of Camp Murphy. Both are now on the National Register of Historic Places.

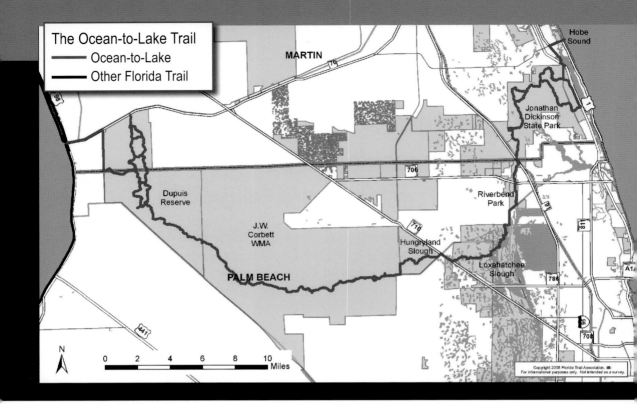

The Ocean-to-Lake Trail
— Ocean-to-Lake
— Other Florida Trail

MARTIN

Hobe Sound

Jonathan Dickinson State Park

Dupuis Reserve

Riverbend Park

J.W. Corbett WMA

706

710

Hungryland Slough

Loxahatchee Slough

786

PALM BEACH

N

0   2   4   6   8   10
                    Miles

Copyright 2008 Florida Trail Association, dtb
For informational purposes only. Not intended as a survey.

On the horizon: more greenways and wildlife corridors

With 11,500 acres, Jonathan Dickinson State Park may seem like ample space in which to roam about. But not necessarily to a panther on the move nor to the kind of hiker-camper who is used to challenges like the Appalachian Trail. For those reasons, *connectivity* is always uppermost in the minds of park managers and it's why JDSP is an important component of the Florida Greenways Commission.

The Commission's goals include preserving a natural environment that links Lake Okeechobee with the Atlantic ocean. Part of it is supporting land acquisitions that add links to the chain. Another part is creating wildlife underpasses across major highways and reducing road noise that can upset migrating animals.

One local entity attempting to put the pieces together in the Palm Beach County area is NENA, the Northeast Everglades Natural Area. It maintains a constantly changing map of trailheads and facilities available in public lands from Lake Okeechobee to the ocean. NENA is run by the Palm Beach County Department of Environmental Resources Management. You can get its latest map by contacting NENA at 561-233-2400 or www.co.palm-beach.fl.us/erm/nena. asp.Another resource is the Florida Trail Association, which actually creates hiking paths in public lands and sponsors several events. Contact FTA at: fta@floridatrail.org or 877-HIKE-FLA

Acknowledgements & Credits

This booklet is no means by one author. It also reflects the comments and criticisms of some two dozen persons who have a real love of and concern for their local state park. They include park managers, rangers, volunteers and the entire board of Friends of Jonathan Dickinson State Park, Inc. It is the latter who have underwritten its cost, and you can be assured that the money you spent for this booklet will be invested in environmental education efforts within the park. — Jim Snyder.

Photos are by the author and editorial associates unless cited below.

Chapter 1: A microcosm of Florida history

p. 6-7. Sue S. Snyder.

p. 8-9. Jim Johnston/Loxahatchee River Historical Society.

p. 10,12. Florida State Photographic Archives.

p. 13. Fishing upriver: Lainhart Family Collection; cypress loggers: Florida State Archives.

p. 14. Loxahatchee River Historical Society

p. 15. Richard Little collection

p. 16-17. Jonathan Dickinson State Park (JDSP) files.

p. 18-19. Camp Murphy map: adapted from U.S. Army Signal Corps map.

p. 19. Aerial view: Loxahatchee River Historical Society

p. 22. Florida State Photographic Archives

p 24. JDSP/William Lund Collection

p. 25. South Florida Water Management District (SFWMD).

p. 26. SFWMD.

p. 27. SFWMD.

Chapter 2: Ecology systems in the park

p. 30. Myrtle oak: Florida Park Service.

p. 31. Rosemary, greenbrier: Ed Weislo/Floridasnature.com; scrub mint: Florida Park Service; dancing lady (orchid): U.S. Dept. of Agriculture.

p. 32. Four-petalled pawpaw: Center for Plant Conservation; Florida scrub-jay, Florida scrub-lizard: Florida Division of Forestry; Red widow spider: U. of Florida Institute of Food and Agricultural Sciences (IFAS); spotted skunk: Florida Fish and Wildlife Conservation Commission.

p. 33. Turkey oak: U. of Florida IFAS.

p. 34. Gopher apple: Floridata.com; blazing star: Florida Park Service; wire grass: U.S. Forest Service; eastern diamond-back rattler: National Geographic Society.

p. 35. Bobwhite: Audubon Society; rufous-sided towhee: flickr.com; cross section drawing: Florida Park Service.

p. 36 Shiny blueberry, white tailed deer: Ed Weislo/floridasnature.com;

p. 37. Deer tongue, gallberry, lopsided Indian grass, tarflower: U. of Florida School of Forest Resources and Conservation; grass-pink: Florida Division of Forestry; Sensitive brier: Missouri State University Dept. of Biology; Bachelor's button: flickr.com

p. 38. Staggerbush: U.S. Dept. of Agriculture; beachberry: Atlas of Florida Vascular Plants; Florida bobcat: Florida International University; coral snake: Florida Museum of Natural History.

p. 39. Toothache grass, maidencane: U.S. Dept. of Agriculture.

p. 40. Hatpin: Florida Federation of Garden Clubs Inc.; stargrass: U. of Florida Institute of Food and Agricultural Sciences; meadow beauty: Florida Park Service; yellow-eyed grass: U.S. Dept. of Agriculture; St. John's wort: U. of Florida IFAS; northern harrier: U.S. Forest Service, USDA; red-winged blackbird: U.S. Geologic Survey.

p. 41. Killdeer: Stetson University; sandhill crane: Southwest Florida Water Management District.

p. 42. Pond cypress: Sue S. Snyder; Southern cricket frog: University of Georgia.

p. 43. Swamp bay: Duke University; Loblolly bay: U. of Florida Institute of Food and Agricultural Sciences. Wood stork: U.S. Fish and Wildlife Service; wood duck: Florida Fish and Wildlife Conservation Commission; swallow tailed kite: Florida Dept. of Environmental Protection.

p. 44. Strand swamp: South Florida Water Management District.

p. 45. Bald cypress: SFWMD; cabbage palm, Ed Weislo/floridasnature.com; red maple: Florida Dept. of Environmental Protection; pond apple: U. of Florida Institute of Food and Agricultural Sciences.

p. 46. Floodplain swamp: Sue S. Snyder; Florida cottonmouth: Florida Museum of Natural History.

p. 47. White ibis: Palm Beach County Water Utilities Dept.; great white heron: Florida Park Service; Florida alligator: Fred Cone.

p. 49. Osprey: Florida Fish and Wildlife Conservation Commission.

p. 50. Mangrove tree crab, fiddler crab: Smithsonian Field Station at Fort Pierce; sea oxeye: flickr.com; mullet: Florida Fish and Wildlife Conservation Commission.

p. 51. Manatee: U.S. Geologic Survey; poison ivy: Ed Weislo/floridasnature.com; poisonwood: U. of Florida Institute of Food and Agricultural Sciences.

Chapter 3: Activities in and around the Park

p. 52. Map: Adapted from Florida Park Service map.

p. 55. Map: Club Scrub.

p. 57-60. Adapted from Florida Park Service maps.

p. 61. Lainhart Dam: South Florida Water Management District.

p. 66. Trapper Nelson site: Adapted from Florida Park Service map.

p. 70. Jupiter Inlet Lighthouse: Jim Johnston/ImageBlast Inc.

p. 71. Dubois House: Loxahatchee River Historical Society

Chapter 4: The Struggle to Remain Wild and Scenic

p. 76. Burn scene: Scott Tedford/Florida Park Service.

p. 77. Ranger with dip torch: Ted Fasoldt, Volunteer, JDSP.

p. 78. Old world climbing fern: U. of Florida Institute of Food and Agricultural Sciences. p. 81. Florida scrub-jay: Florida Division of Forestry.

p. 84. Kayaks atop Trapper Nelson boat shed: Linda Shuster.

p. 85. Bridge across Kitching Creek: Sue S. Snyder.

p. 86. River maps: South Florida Water Management District.

p. 88. Volunteer water sampling: Kristen Ruest/Loxahatchee River Environmental Center.

p. 90. Ocean-to-Lake Trail map: Northeast Everglades Natural Area, Palm Beach County.

Index

Resources

Listed below are some resources for further information on Jonathan Dickinson State Park, the Loxahatchee River and the surrounding area.

Books

Black Gold and Silver Sands: A Pictorial History of Agriculture in Palm Beach County. By James D. Snyder and the Historical Society of Palm Beach County.
> With 250 photos, the dramatic story of a county's emergence from unsettled swampland to modern and abundant farm production in just a few generations.
>> Pharos Books: 2004. 224 pp. $39.95. ISBN 978-0967520056.

Five Thousand Years on the Loxahatchee: A Pictorial History of Jupiter-Tequesta, Florida. By James D. Snyder.
> Over 200 photos and maps illuminate a rich history from the days of the Jeaga Indians to modern times.
>> Pharos Books: 2003. 217 pp. $39.95. ISBN 978-0967520049.

Life and Death on the Loxahatchee, by James D. Snyder.
> The story of Trapper Nelson, a real-life Tarzan who fascinated a generation in South Florida.
>> Pharos Books: 2002. 160 pp. $14.95. ISBN 978-097520063.

A Light in the Wilderness: The Story of Jupiter Inlet Lighthouse & The Southeast Florida Frontier. By James D. Snyder.
> The transition of South Florida from fewer than 600 settlers in 1860 through the Civil War, the age of steamboats and a railroad that would usher in an era of breathtaking population growth.
>> Pharos Books: 2007. 284 pp. $28.95. ISBN 978-0967520018.

Periodicals, Reports, etc.

"The Archeology of Jupiter Inlet and Coastal Palm Beach County." A special issue of *The Florida Anthropologist,* published September-December 2002 by the Florida Anthropological Society, Inc., Tallahassee, FL.

"Northeast Everglades Natural Area: A World-class Destination." August, 2005. 52 pp. Describes the master plan for linking public lands in and around northern Palm Beach County. Published by the Palm Beach County Dept. of Environmental Resources Management, 3323 Belvedere Rd., Bldg. 502, West Palm Beach, FL 33406.

Restoration Plan for the Northwest Fork of the Loxahatchee River," April 2006. 282 pp. An extensive background and blueprint for enhancing fresh water flows to the river's northwest fork, including the portions within JDSP. South Florida Water Management District, Watershed Management Dept., Coastal Ecosystems Division.

"Vascular Plants of Jonathan Dickinson State Park," by Richard E. Roberts, Roy O. Woodbury and John Popenoe. *Florida Scientist,* Vol. 69 No. 4, Fall, 2006. Publisher: The Florida Academy of Sciences, Inc.

"Vegetational Responses to Saltwater Intrusion Along the Northwest Fork of the Loxahatchee River within Jonathan Dickinson State Park," by Richard E. Roberts, Marion Y. Hedgepeth and Taylor R. Alexander. *Florida Scientist,* Vol. 71, No. 4, Autumn 2008. Publisher: The Florida Academy of Sciences, Inc.

Perhaps the best way to keep informed about happenings in the park is to become a member of Friends of Jonathan Dickinson State Park. Better yet, you can be part of the team that makes it happen! Either way, you'll receive free passes for up to 12 park visits during your membership year. You can also take part in several membership socials and special educational events during the year. And you'll receive the organization's quarterly newsletter. Just fill out this form and return it to the address below – or to the ranger station at the main gate.

• •

Friends of Jonathan Dickinson State Park, Inc.
Membership Application
A non-profit community service organization

❑ Lifetime Corporate: $2500   ❑ Lifetime Patron: $1000   ❑ Corporate: $500

❑ Patron: $100   ❑ Family: $25   ❑ Individual: $15

Name: ....

Address: ....

City: .... State: .... Zip ....

Email: .... Phone ....

❑ I am interested in volunteering with the friends.

Friends of Jonathan Dickinson State Park, Inc.
16450 SE Federal Hwy.
Hobe Sound, FL 33455

For more information on the "Friends" please call (561) 744-9814